GRASSROOTS DRAWINGS

1972 – 1978

Peter Veres

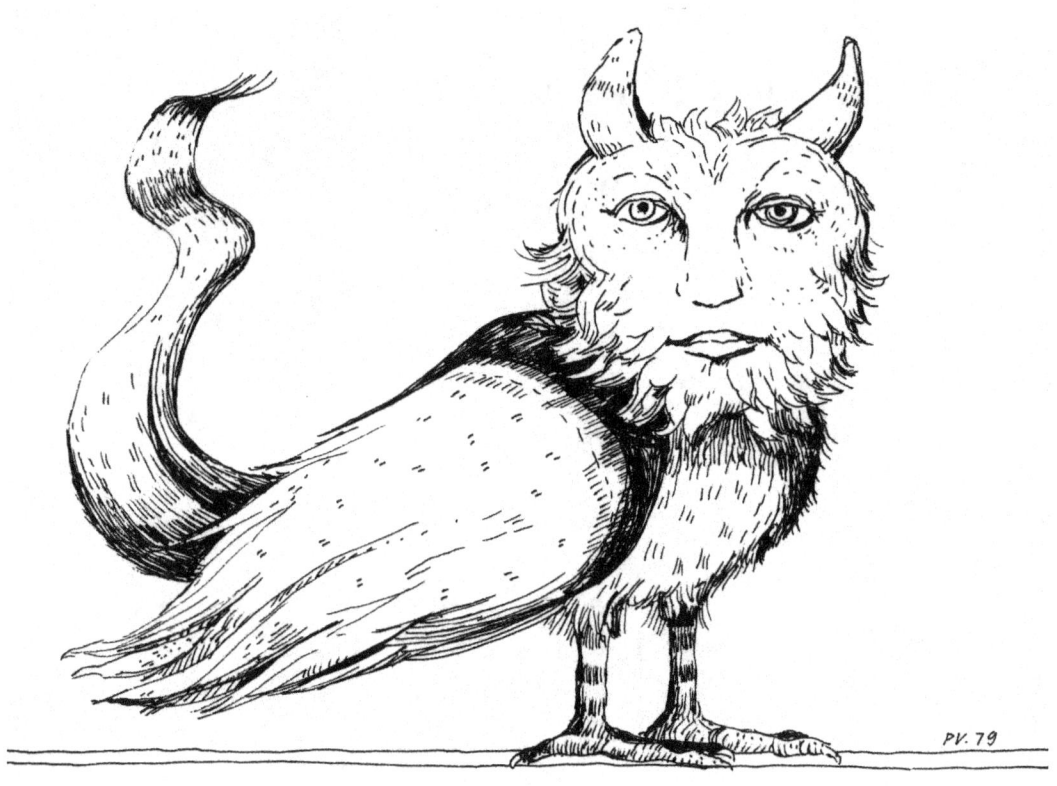

For Ruth, my partner in crime, for better and for worse, who led me to Grassroots.

Copyright © 2020 by Peter Veres
Paperback book
ISBN: 9781655657436

INTRODUCTION

On July 1, 1972 the first issue of **GRASSROOTS : A Berkeley Community Newspaper** was published as a twelve-page tabloid. Its masthead gives the names of eighteen people who created the inaugural issue, and the editorial introduces the paper this way:

What Is Grassroots?

Unless a newspaper serves its community it will fail. The Berkeley left community, on which the Berkeley Monitor and Tribe depended, no longer saw the relevance of either newspaper and therefore did not expend sufficient energy to keep them functioning.

The Monitor was a victim of the large political changes that took place in Berkeley during and following the 1971 municipal elections. The Berkeley Coalition became part of the April Coalition and later, the Coalition. The Monitor editorial staff, for the most part, antedated these organizational changes and did not become involved in the processes and thinking that resulted from them. Instead of capitalizing on the election of the new city council and school board members, the staff only made weak efforts to keep abreast of the political side of issues. Events of council and school board meetings were usually well covered, certainly more thoroughly than in the Berkeley daily. However, the isolation from radical community thinking was reflected in the paper.

The founders of the Monitor hoped to eventually be independent of the Coalition and to establish a traditional left-liberal journal. This rigid direction toward traditional journalism was a factor in the death of the paper. Because of its non-advocate position there were fewer people willing to work on its publication. In fact, it became a liability. Thus the Monitor died.

Grassroots was conceived by a group of Coalition people as an unabashedly political newspaper, communicating the political doings of the Coalition and of Berkeley government. It will also give background and analysis of issues not available through other media. It belongs to the radical community who will be responsible for its publication. We conceive of Grassroots as being the news-organ of the Coalition. As such it will be political and serve the Berkeley left as an aggressive instrument for radical change, and as a means of communication and information sharing between ourselves.

While Grassroots is learning the ropes it will be published monthly. The organizers want the paper to evolve slowly during the summer when fewer people are around. The big push will come in the fall. But we need involvement now. People who can commit themselves to work on layout, distribution, ad sales, photography, graphics, or whatever skills that might be useful in a newspaper are needed and should let Grassroots know.

GRASSROOTS was an independent volunteer collective, unaffiliated with any specific political group. The newspaper reflected the various progressive views of the volunteers who worked on
it at any given time. There was a rotation of editors, and each issue was designed by those who gave their time and effort to it. There was continuity but also change in personnel.

By the time I made my first drawings for Grassroots, for the October 1972 issue, Ruth and several friends were among the people who worked on the paper. I had six drawings in that issue and, until we left Berkeley in 1978, I contributed over a hundred more. The drawings for column logos were printed repeatedly, but I only show them in the first issues in which they appeared.

There were many issues in those six years in which I had no new drawings, which is why there are issue numbers missing in the enclosed sequence. I should note that there were other people who contributed drawings to Grassroots, but I am showing only my own work here.

The drawings I have included were all scanned from old copies of the paper since most of my original drawings were lost, having been pasted up on the galleys we prepared for the printer which were usually tossed when that issue came out. I am presenting the images in black and white, trying to overcome the fading and yellowing gray of the old newsprint and to approach the look of the original drawings.

Where I thought it would help clarify the image I placed the article's headline under the drawing in bold caps. For most of the drawings I also added a clipping from the article or gave a short description or comment on the piece. Political cartoons don't make too much sense when the people and issues they target are unknown or forgotten, but the general thrust of the drawings is still decipherable. Not surprisingly, most of the problems they addressed are still pertinent today: war, racism, corruption and inequality.

Though Grassroots continued publication into 1986, Ruth and I worked on it only through Volume VI, when we left Berkeley in August of 1978. I made all of the drawings shown in this book in the first six years of Grassroots.

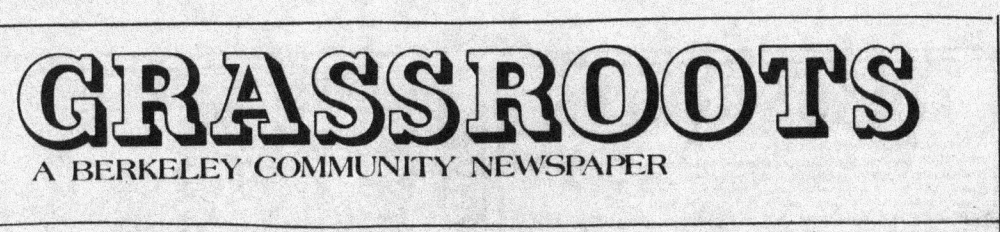

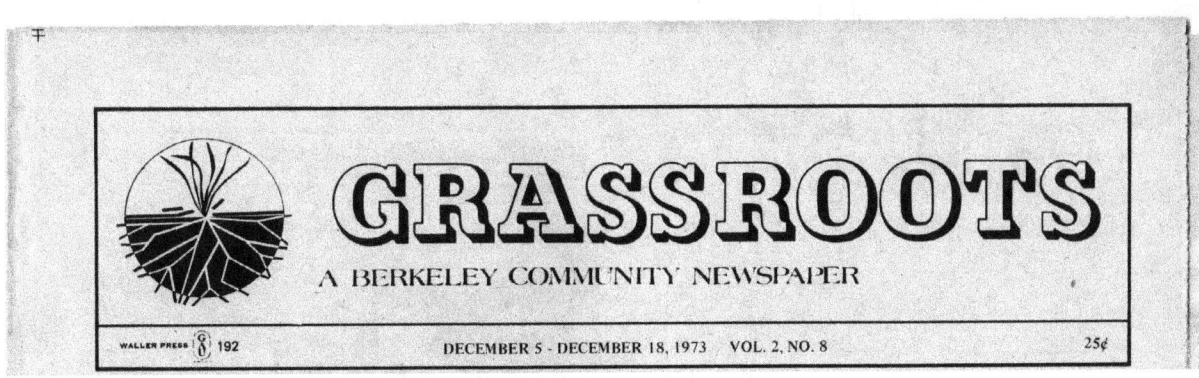

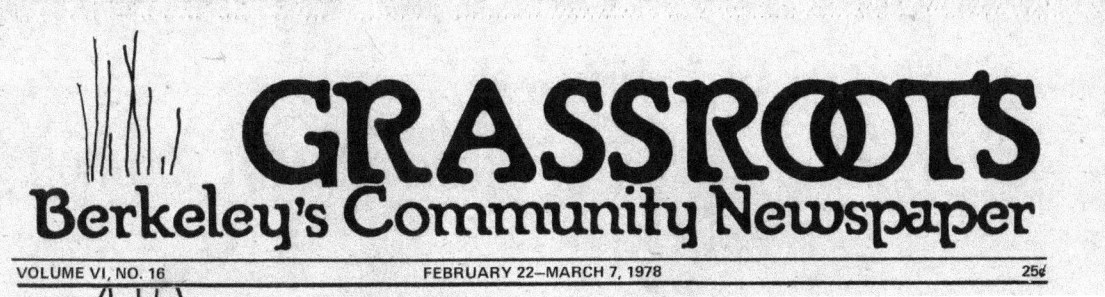

The GRASSROOTS nameplate changed over the first six volumes as shown above.

Vol. I, No. 4   October, 1972

CENTERFOLD   OCTOBER 14 MARCH AND RALLY IN SAN FRANCISCO

GRASSROOTS

A Berkeley Community Newspaper   20 cents

October 1972   Vol. 1 No. 4

State Ballot Issues
A BIRD'S EYE VIEW

This November California voters must consider a stunning array of State propositions. Although several of these measures appear harmless enough, past experience has shown they deserve careful study. For example, Proposition 8 appears as an innocuous "ecology" measure that might help curb pollution. Yet if this issue is approved, it will provide huge tax write-offs for industry which, by encouraging industrial growth, actually increases pollution.

Grassroots discusses the propositions and makes recommendations. We have included a summary of our recommendations for your convenience.

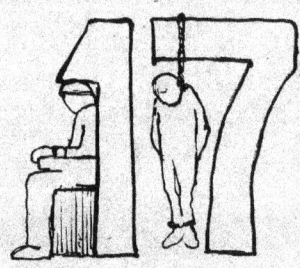

VOTE NO ON THE DEATH PENALTY!

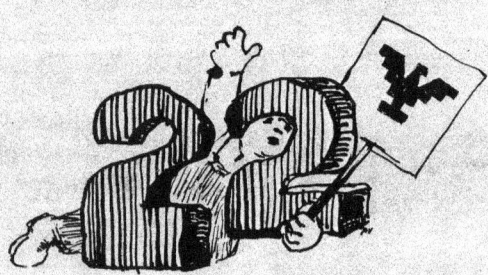

VOTE NO ON THE ANTI-FARM LABOR 22

Proposition 3
Proposition 3 allows the legislature to issue revenue bonds for the purchase, construction, and installation of pollution control facilities. These facilities would then be leased, at low interest (of course), to private companies. The cost of controlling pollution should be borne directly by the company. But companies pass those costs on to the consumer. Someday consumer consciousness will discourage the production of unnecessary items. Until then VOTE NO ON 3.

Proposition 4
The Legislative Reorganization measure (Prop. 4) calls for a two-year session and several procedural reforms. Proponents argue that this issue will streamline operations of the legislature and provide more responsiveness to the public. This remains to be seen! But, because of the two-year session, special interests will have a more difficult time defeating key legislation. This may be the case since the principal opponents are organized interests. WE RECOMMEND YES ON 4.

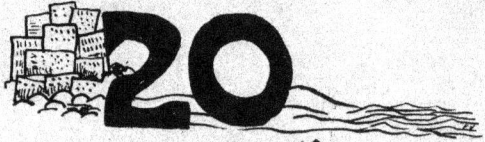

SAVE THE COASTLINE - VOTE YES ON 20

Proposition 1
Proposition 1, if passed, will provide $160 million for major construction, acquisition of equipment, and purchase of sites for community colleges. Junior college systems are governed locally and tend to be more responsive to community pressure than the two state-wide university systems. Locally controlled colleges need encouragement. Yet Berkeley and Northwest Oakland have been 'ripped-off' by the Peralta Junior College District. No Berkeley campus has been built as promised and Grove St. is being phased out. Peralta administrators would use the revenue from this bond to construct a "multipurpose facility" on the Feather River College campus in Plumas Co. and a gym at Alameda College. Athletic equipment would also be purchased. The old Grove St. campus (formerly Merritt) would not receive a dime. Until the Peralta board is returned to the people, WE URGE A NO VOTE ON BOND ISSUES FOR THIS DISTRICT.

Proposition 2
The University's Health Science Facilities Bond (Proposition 2) issue appears routinely on every ballot (look for it on the Rent Control Board Ballot!). This bond would provide the kind of facilities that every medico and every potential medico (and other assorted pretenders) assumes to be its inalienable right. Our medical system stinks and providing these chumps with more labs and classrooms just helps perpetuate their smelly system. When our medical people get it together, then we will provide the bread. Until we have socialized, community medicine, screw it! We will just be breeding yachts. VOTE NO.

Proposition 5
Proposition 5 authorizes school boards to initiate and carry on any programs or activities which do not conflict with state law. The original legislation on this measure was passed by the legislature but vetoed by Reagan. It allows for more community control of the school system and opponents argue that the State Department of Education will lose "effective control over irresponsible programs." Right on! VOTE YES.

Proposition 6
This measure (Prop. 6) would modernize the State Constitution in line with recommendations of the Constitution Revision Commission. It involves the setting of state boundaries, and concerns suits against the state, and salaries and term of office of state officials. If this issue passes it should be easier to change the term of office of appointed officials, i.e., Board of Regents. VOTE YES.

Proposition 7
Proposition 7 changes the minimum age for voting, incorporates the requirement for open presidential primaries, and removes the details regarding literacy and residency. This is a change in the constitution. Opponents argue that the residence requirement of 30 days would let transients (meaning students) control cities and counties, making it harder for the Chambers of Commerce and Boards of Realtors to control development projects, zoning laws, etc. VOTE YES.

continued on page 16

NO on M

This was the first issue of Grassroots in which my drawings appeared.

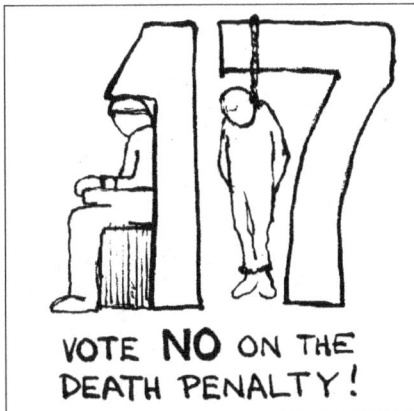
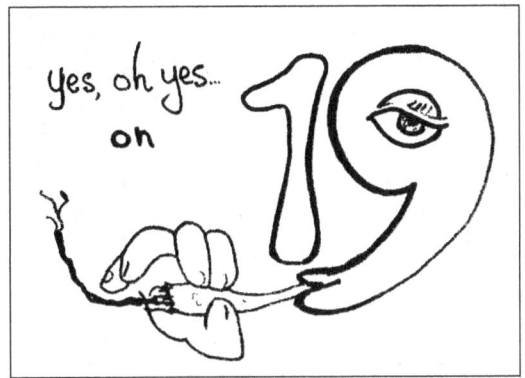
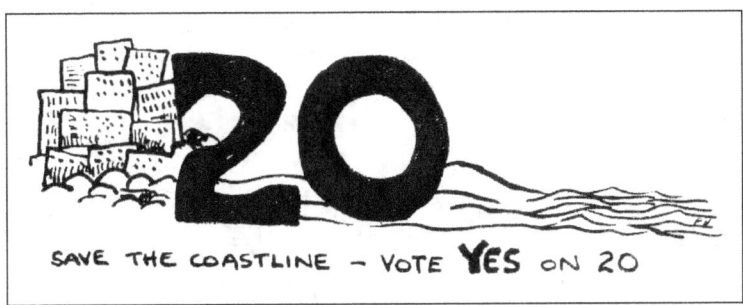
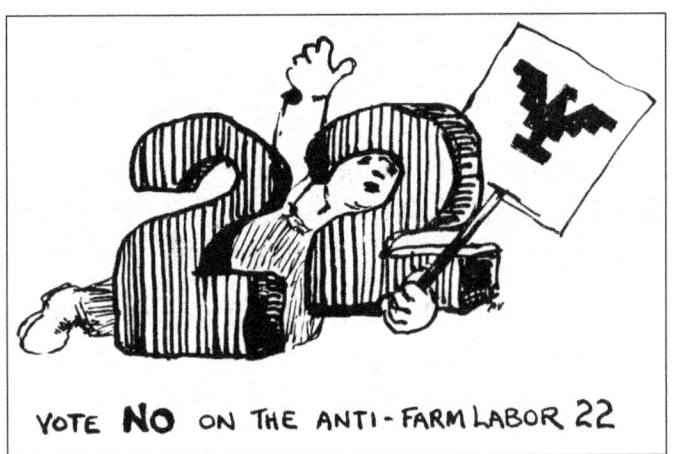

> This November California voters must consider a stunning array of State propositions. Although several of these measures appear harmless enough, past experience has shown they deserve careful study. For example, Proposition 8 appears as an innocuous "ecology" measure that might help curb pollution. Yet if this issue is approved, it will provide huge tax write-offs for industry which, by encouraging industrial growth, actually increases pollution.
>
> *Grassroots* discusses the propositions and makes recommendations. We have included a summary of our recommendations for your convenience.

I illustrated four of the propositions Grassroots was most emphatic about. The captions are enough to indicate the substance of the recommendations.

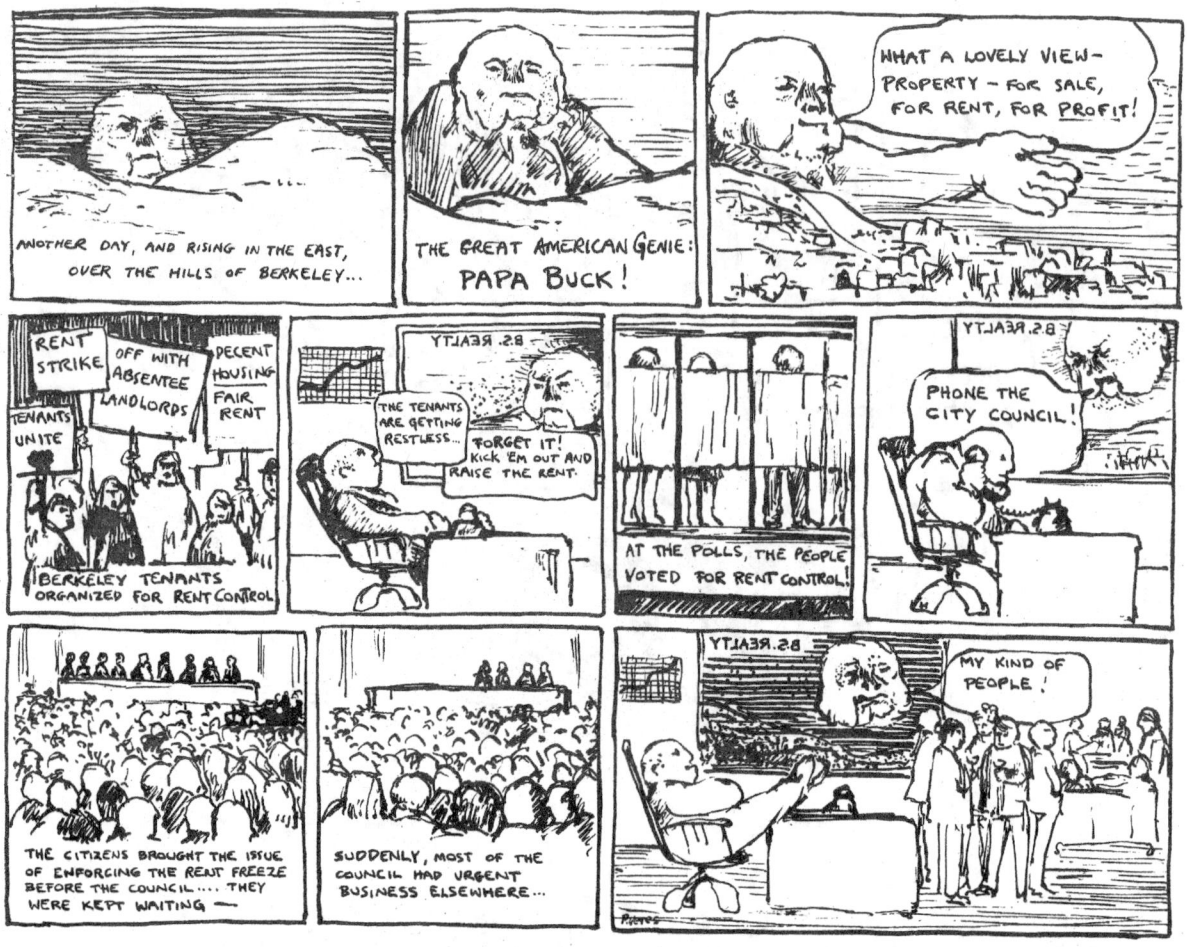

This was my only comic strip layout for Grassroots. It featured Papa Buck, my imagined figure of a powerful genie behind the property interests in Berkeley. Since I had to reduce the image, in the interest of legibility the texts of the panels are given below:

ANOTHER DAY, AND RISING IN THE EAST, OVER THE HILLS OF BEREKELY…

THE GREAT AMERICAN GENIE : PAPA BUCK !

WHAT A LOVELY VIEW – PROPERTY – FOR SALE, FOR RENT, FOR <u>PROFIT</u> !

BERKELEY TENANTS ORGANIZED FOR RENT CONTROL

B.S REALTY   THE TENANTS ARE GETTING RESLESS…
    FORGET IT ! KICK 'EM OUT AND RAISE THE RENT.

AT THE POLLS, THE PEOPLE VOTED FOR RENT CONTROL !

PHONE THE CITY COUNCIL !

THE CITIZENS BROUGH THE ISSUE OF ENFORCING THE RENT FREEZE BEFORE THE COUNCIL…
    THEY WERE KEPT WAITING –

SUDDENLY, MOST OF THE COUNCIL HAD URGENT BUSINESS ELSEWHERE…

MY KIND OF PEOPLE !

Vol. I, No. 5   November, 1972

GRASSROOTS HEALTHCARE SUPPLEMENT

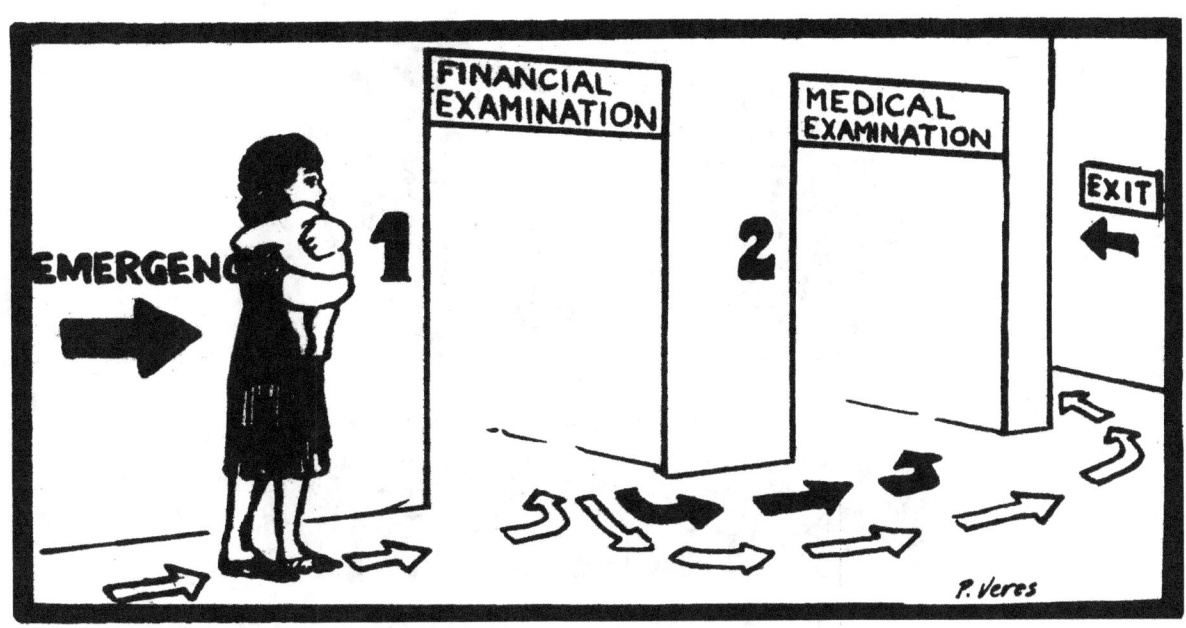

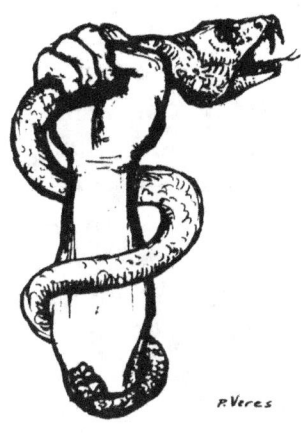

EMERGENCY

More than 2,000 people use Herrick Hospital's emergency room each month. For those with cash in their pockets or Medi-Cal, Medicare, or private health insurance cards in their wallets, treatment is subject only to the "usual" delays. But until recently many people without cash or eligibility cards in hand suffered long delays or denial of treatment in accord with *hospital policy*.

Until the summer of 1971 Berkeley residents and visitors had to deal individually with this problem and others in finding adequate emergency medical care.

Herrick refused, and MCHR brought the matter to the City Council.

Some 250 people overflowed the Council chambers in November 1971 for a public hearing on Herrick's emergency room. One person told how his treatment for painful second degree burns had been delayed until he could guarantee payment; another described a 7-hour wait while bleeding from the rectum; a third told of being turned away while hemorrhaging and cramping from an intra-uterine device inserted by Herrick the previous day.

Herrick's administrators denied

This was a long piece on health care services and their problems in Berkeley. The above is a clip from the tops of the first two columns to get a sense of the article.

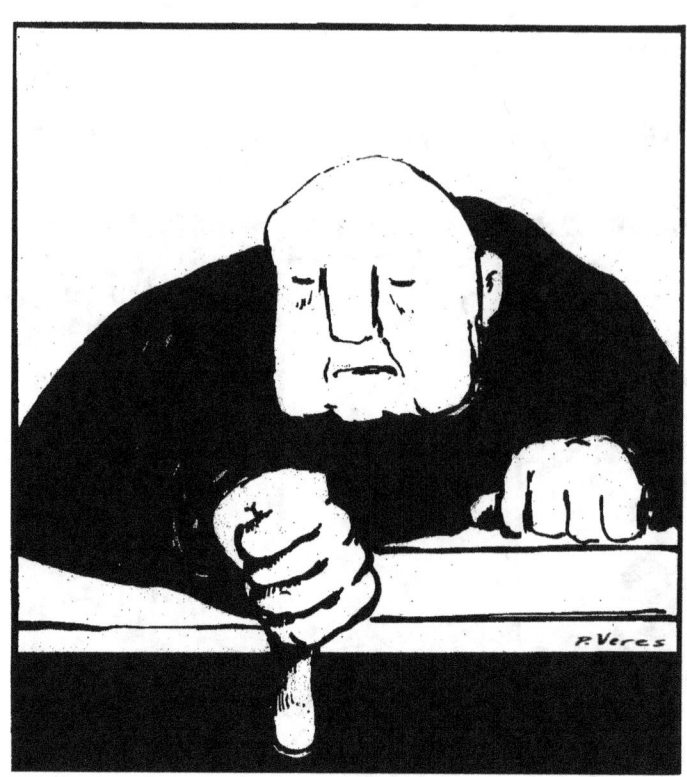

ACTIVIST LAWYER DENIED PRACTICE

After a while the waiting begins to get on my nerves. It's now been exactly two years since I learned that I has passed the California Bar Examination in August 1970, and I still don't know whether I will ever be allowed to practice law.

The case is now before the California Supreme Court. The last briefs were filed on October 24, but the Court still hasn't let us know whether they will even consider my appeal from the Committee of Bar Examiner's decision that I am not morally fit to join Joe Alioto, Evelle Younger, and Richard Nixon as an officer of the court.

The reasons given by the Committee of Bar Examiner for excluding me were flimsy, and my lawyers — Mal Burnstein, Marshall Krause, Barry Winograd and Frank McTernan — think we will win in the State Supreme Court. But the Bar Examiners have already won. For the past two years my life has been dominated by the uncertainty of the situation. This has made all planning impossible as well as resulting in some subtle and probably not so subtle changes in my personality, relationships with other people, and world outlook.

A long piece by Dan Siegel, Berkeley activist and UC Law School graduate. Denied a license to practice law by the State Bar Examiners because of his political activism, on his appeal the California Supreme Court overruled the State Bar and found that Siegel possessed the requisite "moral character" to practice law. Siegel practices employment and labor law in Oakland, CA.

ECONOMIC POLITICS OF BERKELEY

The struggle for political control of Berkeley has so far left one area of most of our lives relatively untouched: the way we make a living. While the city government itself provides some jobs, the political decisions made at City Hall or in the streets have only occasional or indirect effect on everyone's woraday lives. The types of jobs, the condition of work, and the size of our incomes are determined primarily in a labor market where all of us still function as atomized individuals, subject to the whims of employers and fluctuations in the regional and national economy.

This article is the first in an intermittent series which will examine the political economy of Berkeley; its employment, income and wealth ownership patterns and the relationship between economic power and political power. In this first overview of the Berkeley economy, we will look at what types of jobs are available, who the main employers are, and an indication of where power lies.

I don't know why this drawing was used with this long article. It seems that I flipped the coin of Patrick Henry's famous "Give me Liberty, or Give me Death!" and came up with both choices.

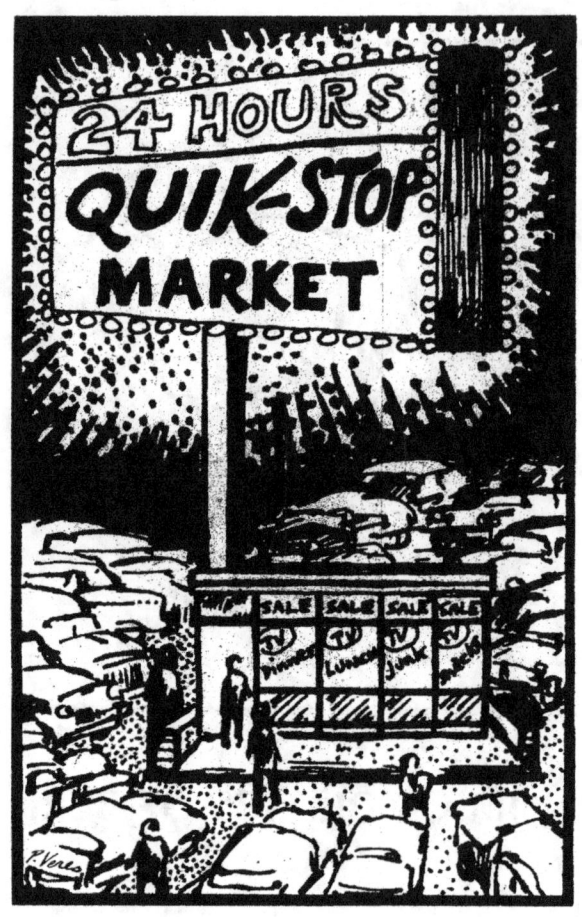

QUIK STOP – STOPPED QUICK

Neighbors from the Monterey-Hopkins area successfully blocked the issuance of a use permit for the construction of a Quik Stop market/self-service gas station. The proposed site, where Monterey runs into Hopkins, is already serviced by a gas station and two food markets. The addition of a "junk food" store was not a welcome prospect to the neighborhood.

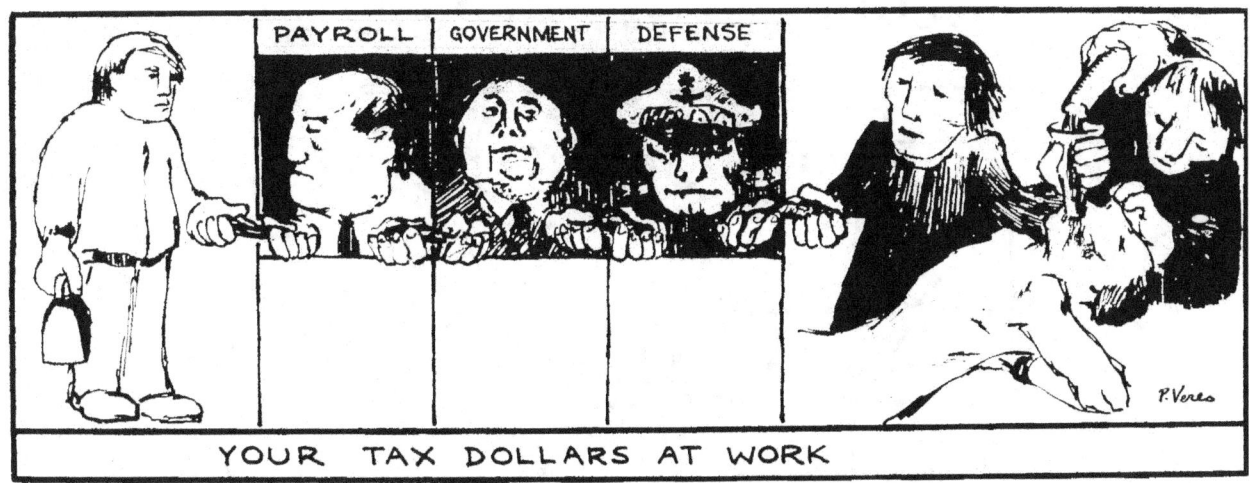

AMERICA'S ASIAN AUSCHWITZ

Reports of mass arrests in Vietnam, torture of political prisoners and persistent rumors of wholesale liquidation of opponents of the Thieu regime emphasize the failure of the current peace talks to end the suffering in Vietnam.

How many prisoners is unknown.

The Government of South Vietnam admits to 30,000 prisoners. The Department of Defense gives the figure of 100,000. Amnesty International and Overseas Vietnamese Buddhists report something over 2,000,000 political prisoners. Don Luce, a journalist with twelve years' experience in Vietnam, gave in Congressional testimony the figure of 400,000 prisoners, 100,000 of them political prisoners.

The Saigon Committee for the Reform of Prisons reports nearly two percent of the population of South Vietnam is political prisoners.

The *San Francisco Chronicle* of August 5, 1972, reported arrests approaching 14,000 civilians per month since April of this year. Sydney Schanberg in the *New York Times,* August 13, 1972, wrote that prisoners were routinely tortured at detention centers before being sent to Con Son. "Some said water had been forced down their mouths until they nearly drowned, while others told of electric prods used on sensitive parts of the body, of fingernails pulled out. and fingers mashed."

Who are the prisoners? They are religious leaders, both Catholic and

For his later reports from Cambodia, Sydney Schanberg won the Pulitzer Prize in 1976. His book on the horrors of that war became the basis of the 1984 film *The Killing Fields*.
Following the money: in the drawing, part of a worker's pay is withheld as taxes, it goes to the Government, is handed to the Defense Department, which pays for war and torture in Vietnam.

Vol. I, No. 7   January 20, 1973

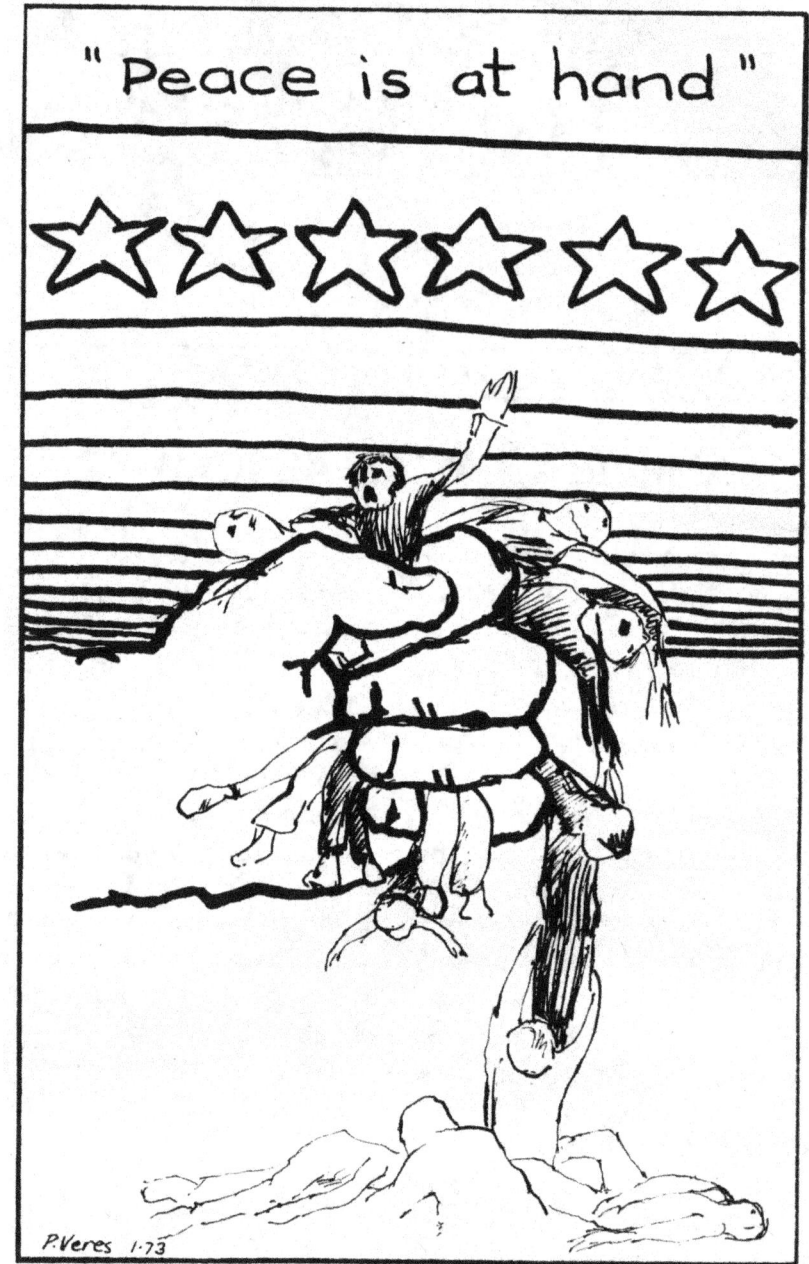

There was no article about the war, but on the front page there was call for a demonstration for peace on the day of Nixon's inauguration for his second term – the term he did not finish.

DEMONSTRATE JAN. 20
INAUGURATION DAY
NIXON MUST SIGN PEACE AGREEMENT!

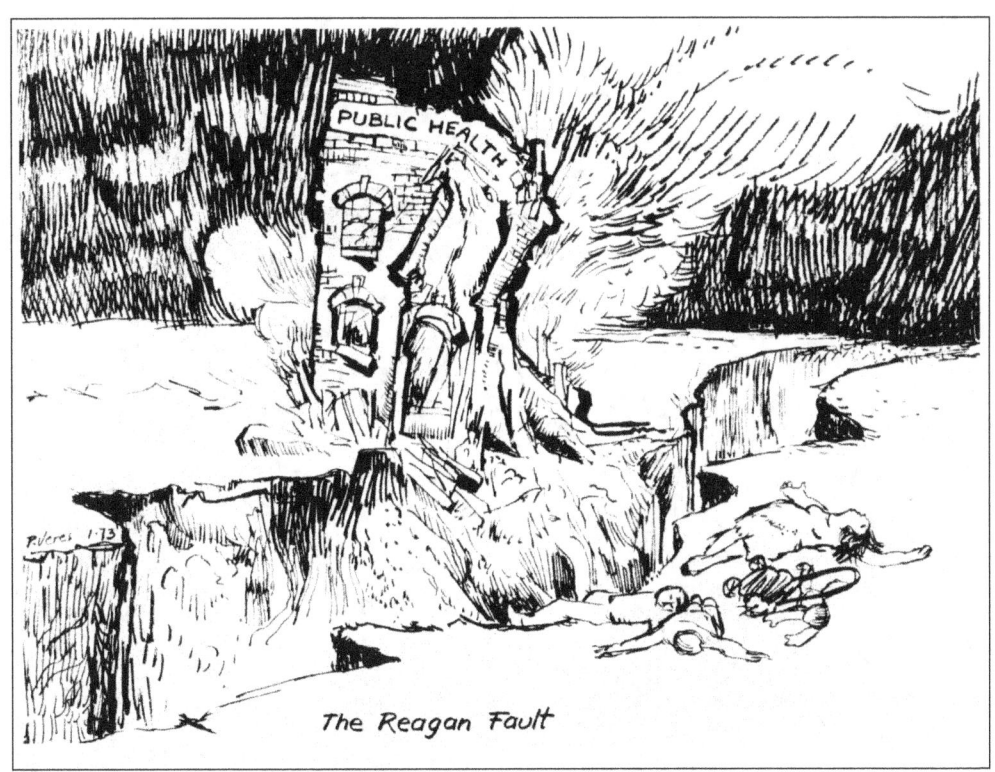
The Reagan Fault

PUBLIC HEALTH MOVE THREATENS JOBS

The entire East Bay State legislative delegation has joined the swelling ranks of opposition to the transfer of State Department of Public Health employees from Berkeley to Sacramento, as proposed by the Reagan administration.

The move to Sacramento would be part of a Reagan "reorganization" plan which will combine the former Departments of Mental Hygiene, Health Care Services and Public Health in a giant Health Department headquartered in Sacramento.

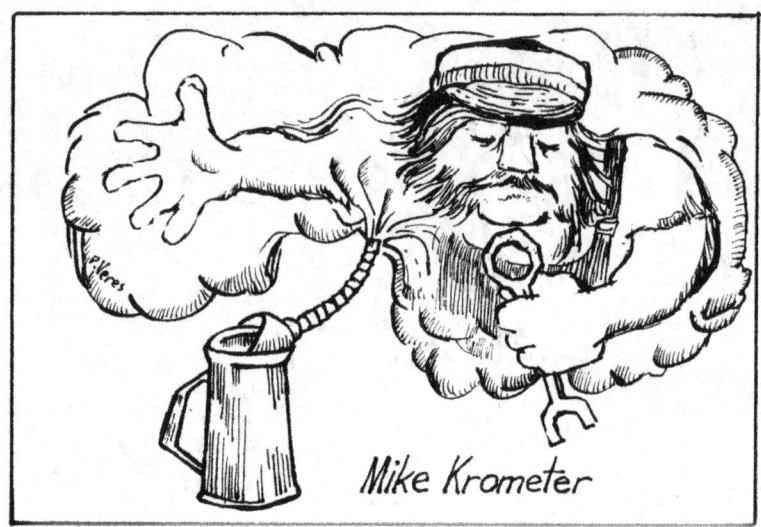

Doug Brown was one of the major workers on Grassroots, and here he introduced his column with his nom de plume, Mike Krometer, to give automotive advice "with the idea that it'll save you a few bucks and many head and heartaches". Mike Krometer made his appearance five years before Click and Clack, the brothers Magliozzi, began their radio show in Boston in 1977.

In Vol. I, No.10 this logo changed to the configuration below, which was kept until Vol. II, No. 10, when I redrew the oil can genie to give it a likeness of Doug himself. (page 61)

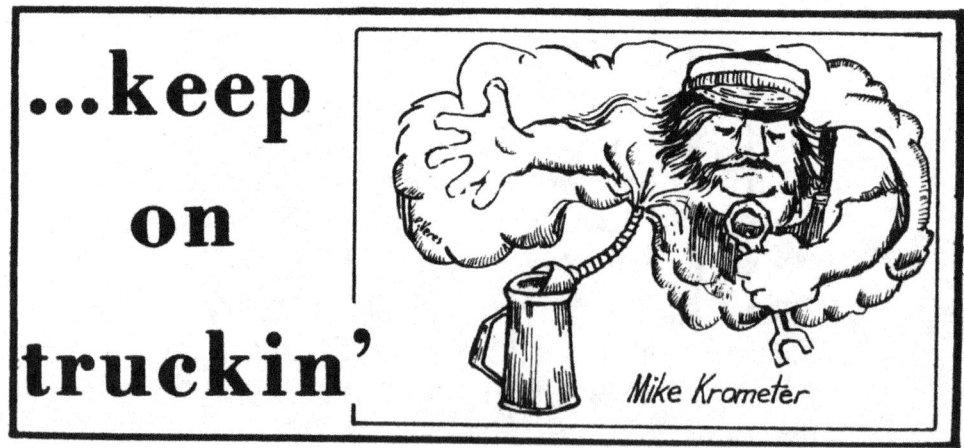

Uncle John's Band

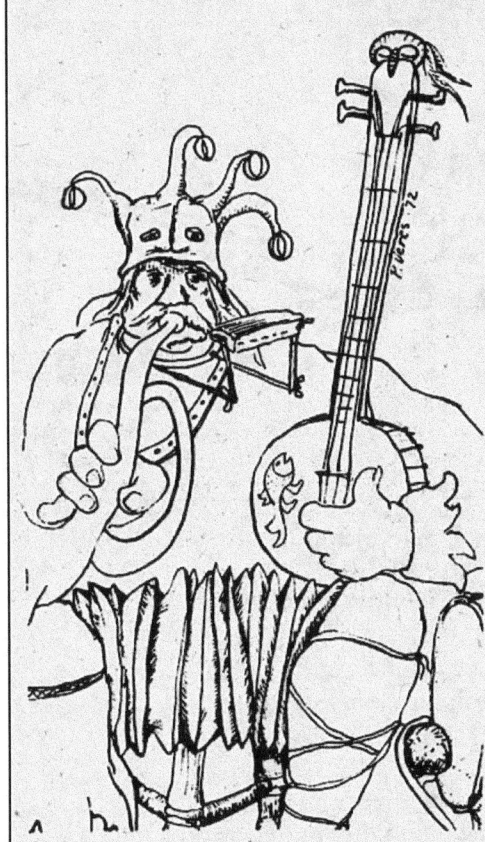

The return of Toni Brown formerly of the Joy of Cooking, to local live performance last month marked an important event in the Berkeley music scene. She and Terri Garthwaite, lead singer for the Joy of Cooking, were back together again for a fine evening of music at Freight and Salvage. Even though it was a Thursday, the small club was packed.

A bit of history: The Joy of Cooking has been the most important, and widest known, Berkeley-based band since Country Joe and the Fish. They cut three albums (Joy of Cooking, Closer to the Ground, and Castles), did some national touring, and performed at most of the larger halls in the Bay Area. They had a strong local following, and consistently filled local clubs with good rocking music.

Last spring, Toni Brown, singer, piano player, and songwriter, left the Joy of Cooking to write and work independently. The Joy has continued around Garthwaite, without Brown and bassist Jeff Nabors. Part of their distinctive sound — the way the two women's voices worked and improvised with each other — was gone.

UNCLE JOHN'S BAND was a column by C.C. Otter, begun in this issue. The name comes from the Grateful Dead song first recorded in 1970.
On the right is the full image which appeared in later columns.

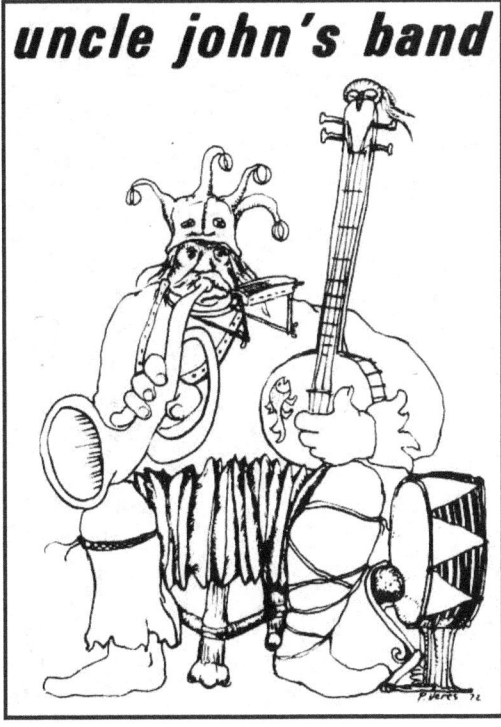

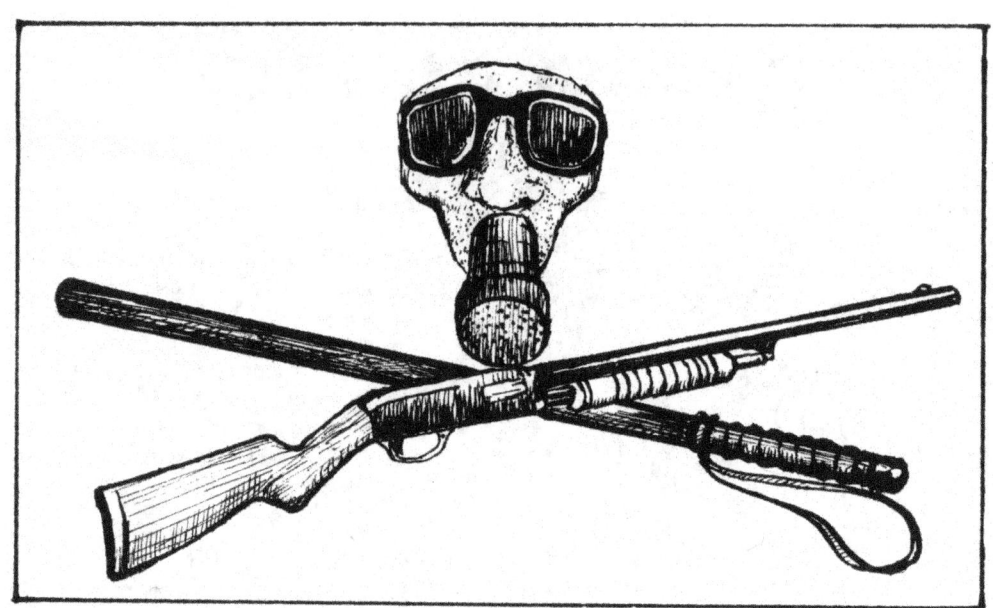

P.I.G. REPORT

On December 22, Donovan Leighton an Oakland policeman, and a former Berkeley Police trainee, came in plainclothes to the Police Issue Group's regular meeting at the Berkeley Black Caucus office on Adeline. He failed to identify himself throughout the meeting and on the sign-up sheet listed only his name and neglected the space for listing "affiliated organization." Only at the end of the meeting was Johnnie Porter able to expose him as a former Berkeley police trainee and as a present Oakland policeman. When asked about his intentions, he said he had come "to find out the thinking of the group and of the people there." When pressed with further questions, he abruptly left the meeting.

Grassroots has since learned that policeman Leighton reported on the meeting to other Oakland policemen, and presumably to the Berkeley Police Department. Since it would be strange for Oakland to be conducting political surveillance in Berkeley, probably Leighton was approached by the Berkeley Police Intelligence Unit to infiltrate the meeting and possibly become a member of the group.

The Police Issue Group (P.I.G.) was a Berkeley neighborhood organization concerned with police conduct. This report was about an undercover cop spying on them at their meeting.

One of the perennial fundraising events in the life of a community organization. I have to say here that the only way we were able to produce professional looking lettering in those days was either to be a calligrapher, which I was not, or to use the Letraset transfer letters pressed individually onto paper to make words, which was a tedious operation. I opted for crude hand lettering… good enough for who it was for.

All of the Grassroots headlines were made with Letraset in the years we worked there, and all the typeset copy and images, including photos, were hand pasted onto the heavy cardstock galleys for printing. These were then hand-delivered to the printer, Warrens Waller Press, a union shop in South San Francisco.

Vol. I, No. 8   February 14, 1973

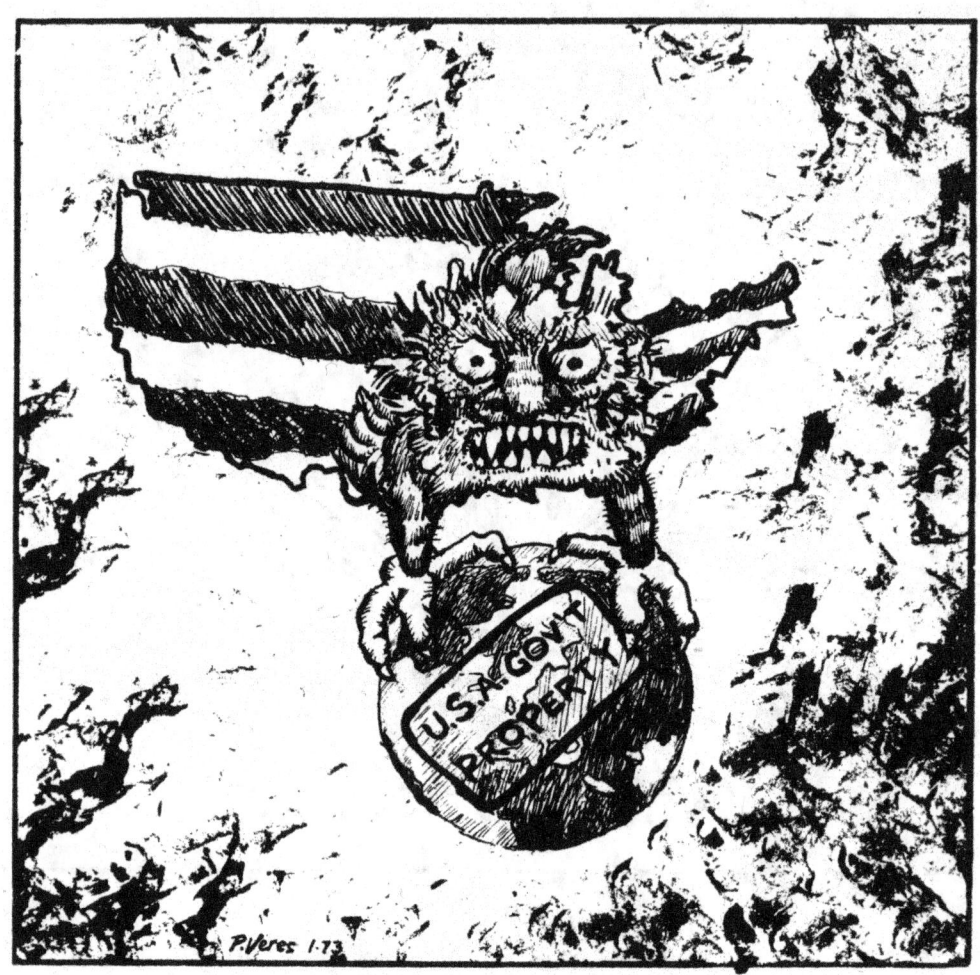

END OF WHICH WAR?

We in the Grassroots Collective share a sense of relief that the signing of the Peace Treaty has brought an end to the wholesale American destruction and slaughter in Vietnam. The real victory belongs to the Vietnamese people; it was their determined resistance which finally defeated American designs for control of their country. We believe that the continued resistance to the war policy by the American peace movement and world public opinion helped to end that war.

Last week American bombers flew 125 sorties daily over Laos from bases in Thailand. The Pentagon continues to use our taxes to wage full-scale war elsewhere in Southeast Asia. American imperialism created Vietnam and continues to oppress people struggling for liberation in Africa, Asia, the Middle East and Latin America.

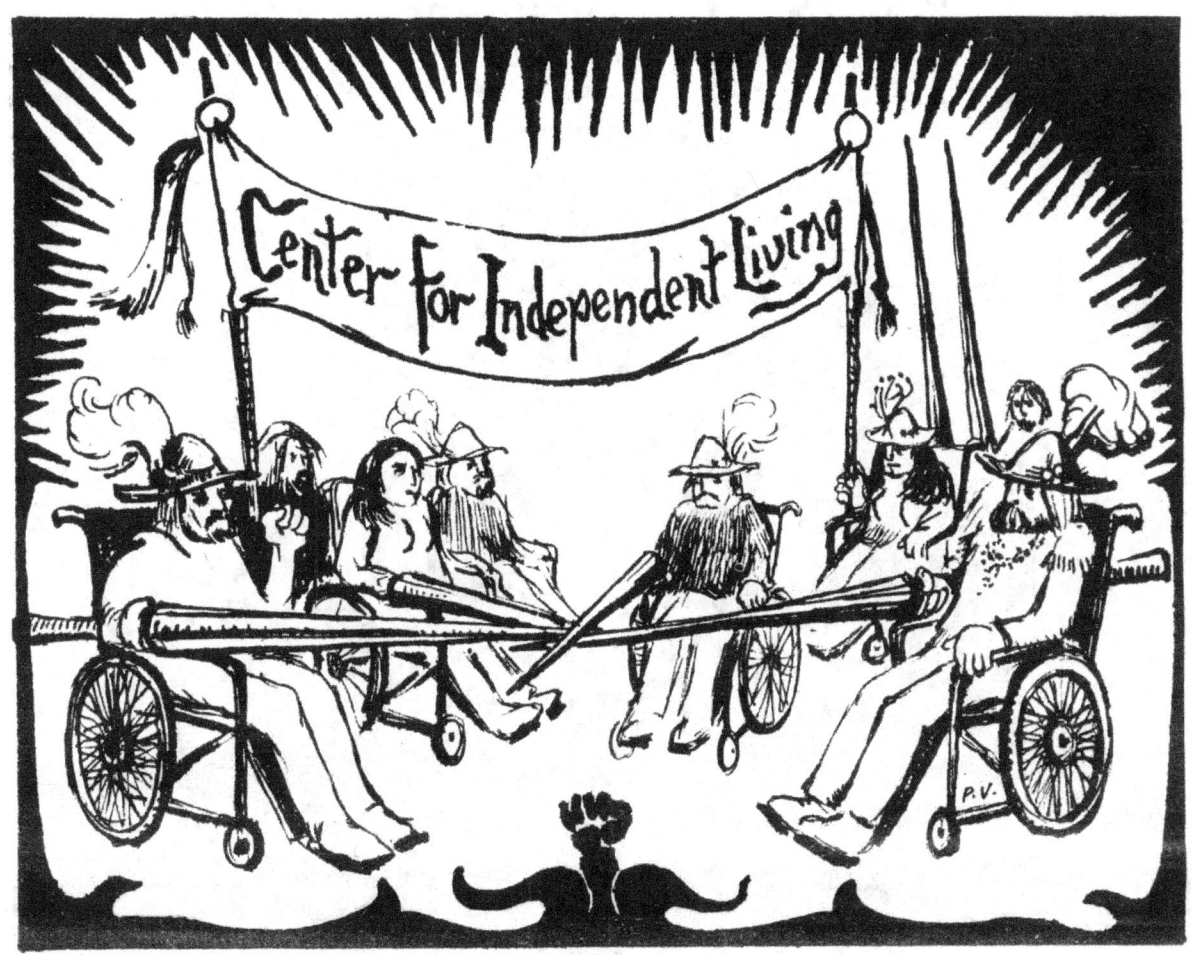

DISABLED DEMAND SELF-DETERMINATION

This was an article written by Ed Roberts who started the disability rights movement at the University of California as a quadriplegic student and later founded the Center for Independent Living in Berkeley in 1972.

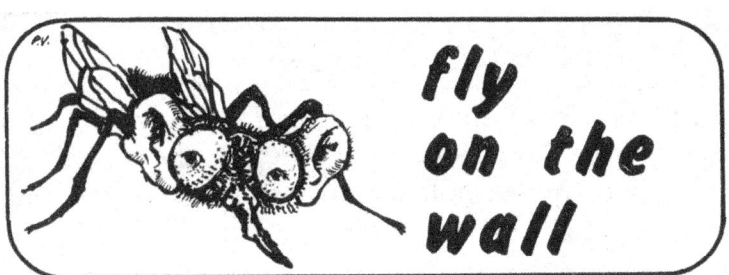 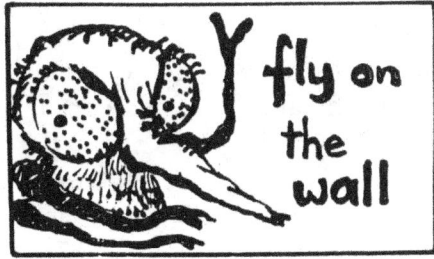

This was a section with short reports and comments on political goings-on in Berkeley. My logo was used in many issues, first the one on the left and later the one on the right from May 1974.

Vol. I, No. 9   March–April, 1973

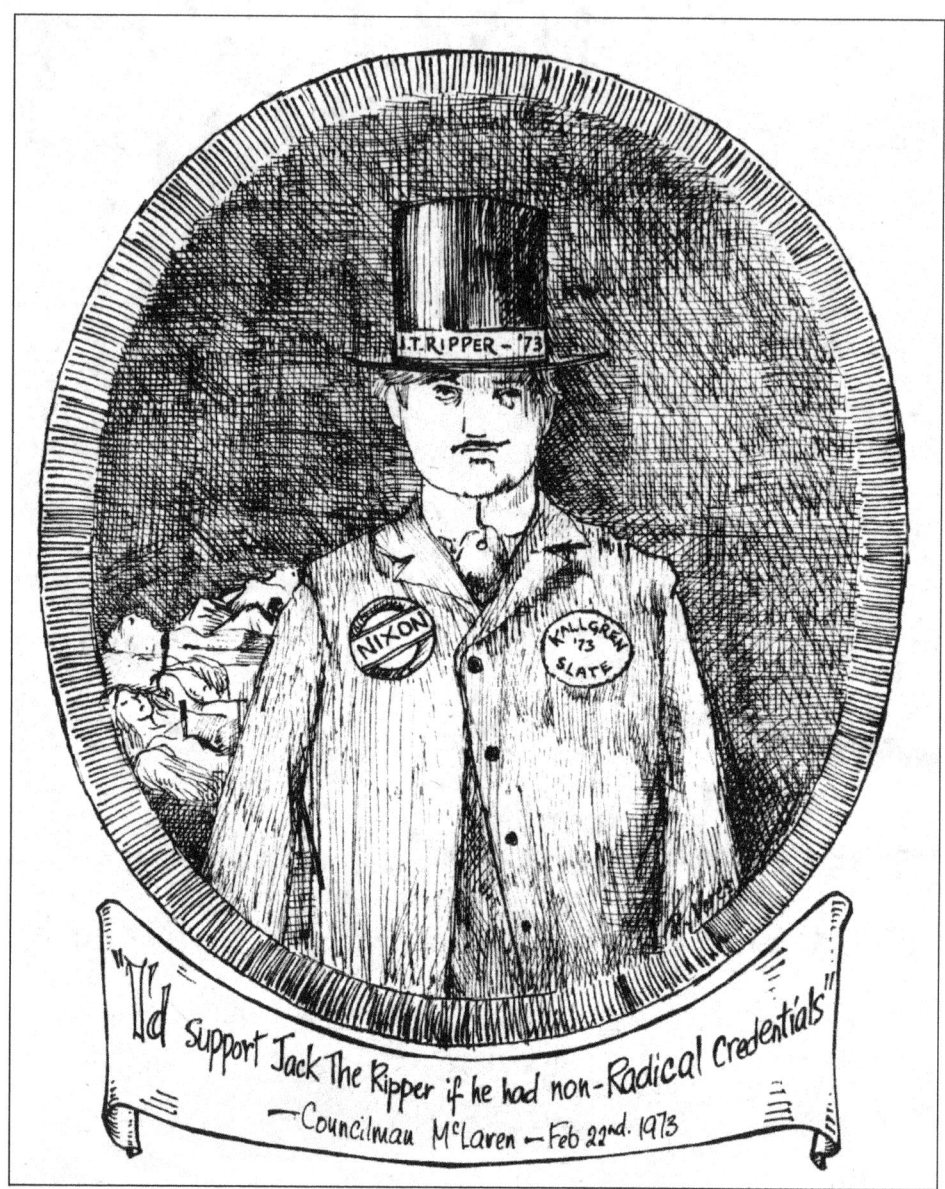

Although this drawing was on the editorial page, Councilman McLaren is only mentioned briefly in the article on page 13 of this issue, the one about the Berkeley Four illustrated with my next image. I don't know where I got the quote, and I doubt that my Jack the Ripper had any resemblance to Mr. McLaren, but this gent with his political buttons looks like a dandy bad guy in an old-fashioned style.

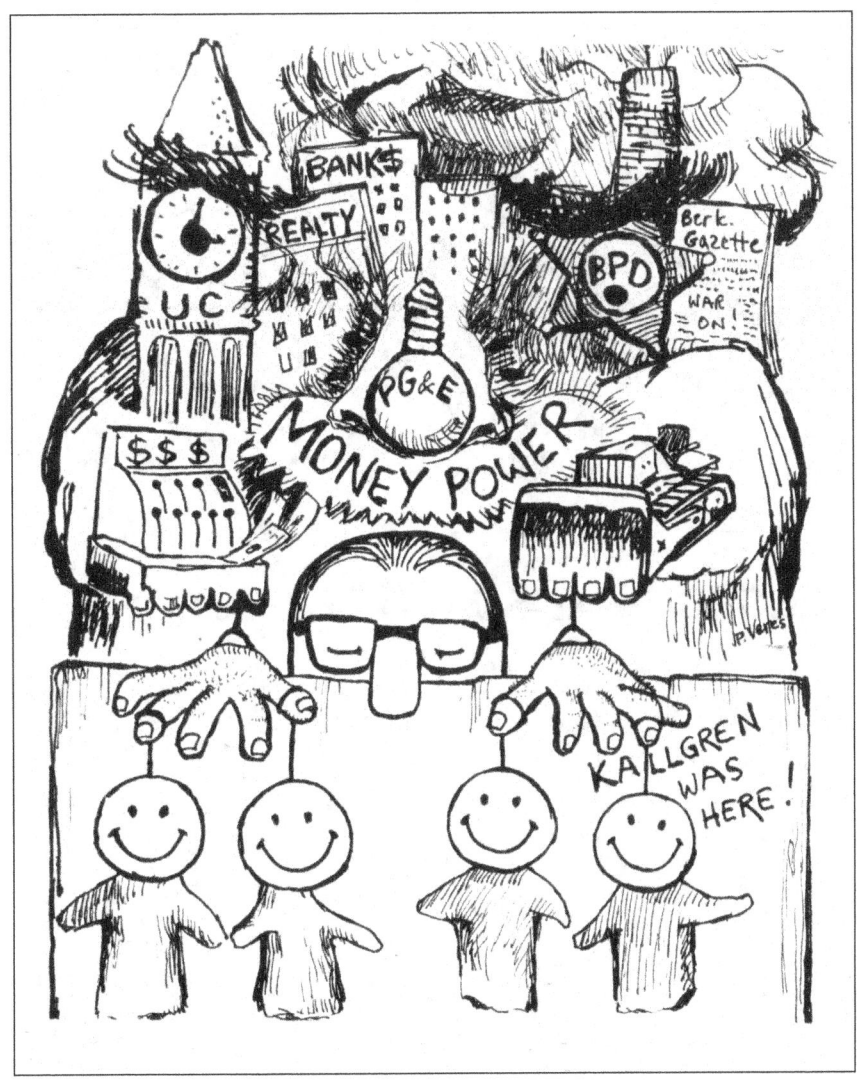

WHO ARE THE BERKELEY FOUR?

Ed Kallgren was a Berkeley City Councilman, known for his connections to the moneyed interests. Quite a different drawing from Jack the Ripper, this was more the style of my political cartoons. None too subtle in depicting the powers behind Kallgren and his four cohorts on the Council, but I liked drawing his face in the "Killroy Was Here" pose of the classic WW II graffiti.

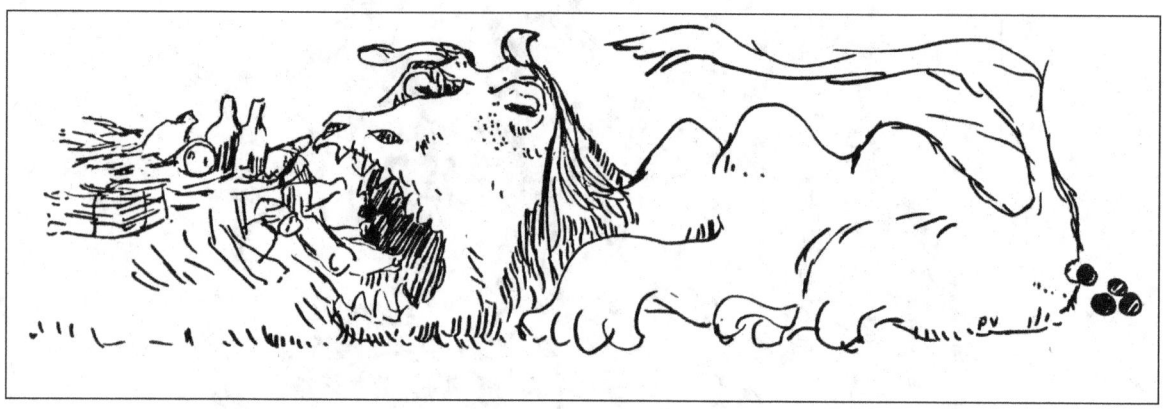

ECOLOGICAL SURVIVAL PROPOSALS

The article was by a member of Berkeley Ecology/Action, and the proposals included Transportation, Solid Waste Management, Land Use and People, meaning people taking responsibility for the environment. My proposal was an organic solution: a recycling beast. As with some of my other cartoons, this one was not received with great favor by everyone in Grassroots. Perhaps it was the poop.

Vol. I, No. 10   April, 73

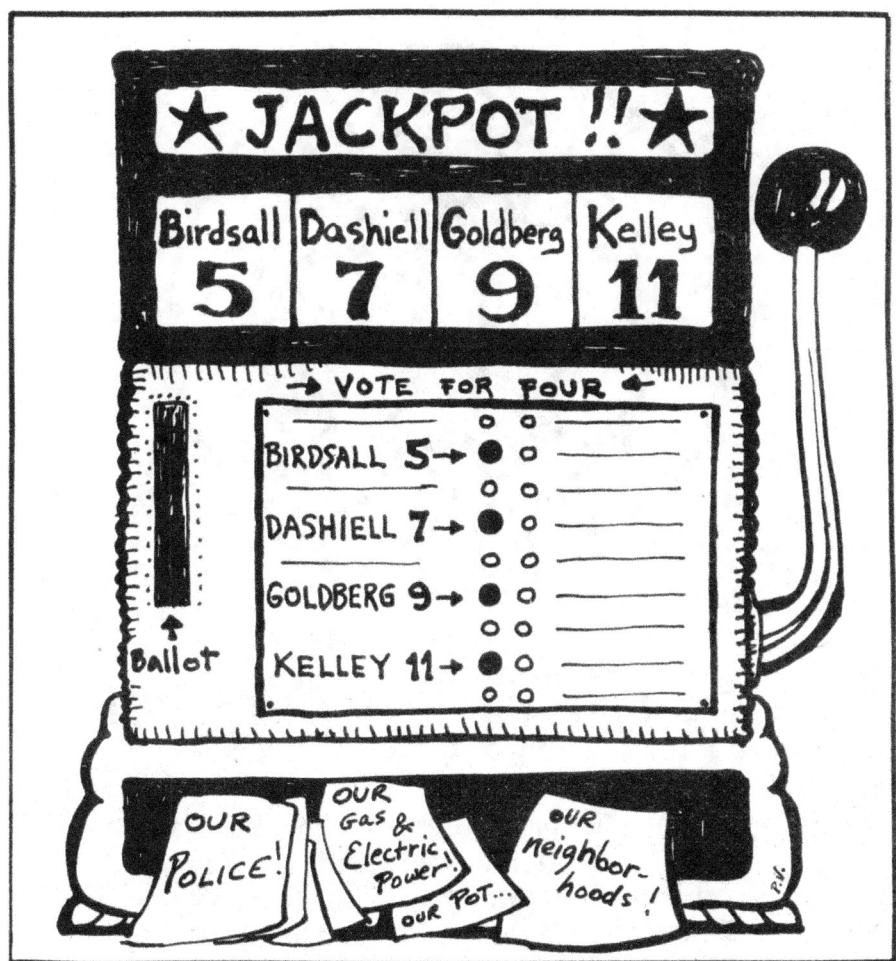

VOTE SLATE

The editorial was a call to vote for the slate of candidates put forth by Berkeley's progressive April Coalition and change the balance of power from the current conservative majority on the City Council. I'm not sure how appropriate my choice of this image was for the local election process at that time, or if it raised any hackles. The suggestion of casino gambling and money and chance is not exactly an ideal for democratic elections. But it certainly seems pretty close to today's election process.

Vol. I, No. 11   May, 1973

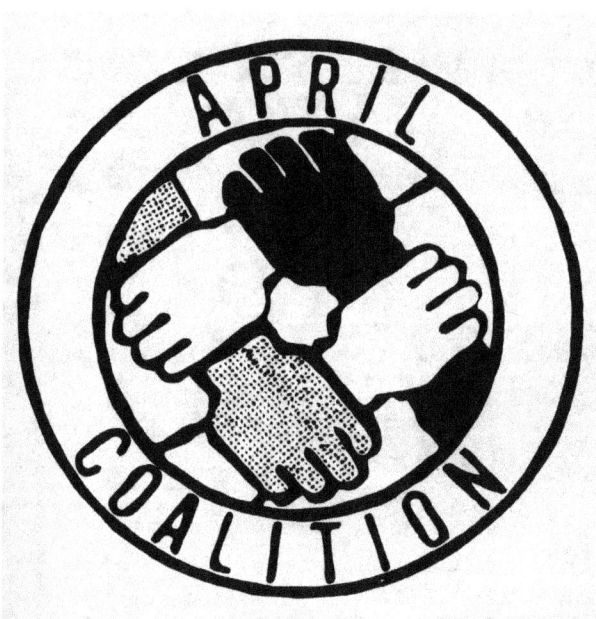

COALITION FUTURE – FIVE VIEWPOINTS

On this page Grassroots presents a series of short interviews with Coalition workers. They are: Bill Sokol, Veronika Fukson, E. Woo, and Cynthia George. The following questions were asked of all of them: What do you think of the outcome of the elections in relation to 1) The Coalition campaign and its internal problems (such as the Miller endorsement controversy); 2) The Berkeley Four campaign; 3) The political situation in Berkeley? Is there a future for the Coalition as an ongoing organization, and if so, how do you envision the functions and the structure of this organization?

Berkeley's April Coalition was an umbrella group of different leftist political groups with different agendas which tried to get a slate of candidates elected to the City Council to offset its control by the conservative majority. I'm not sure why I drew four hands, except to indicate the possible strength in unity if these groups could work together instead of indulging in infighting.

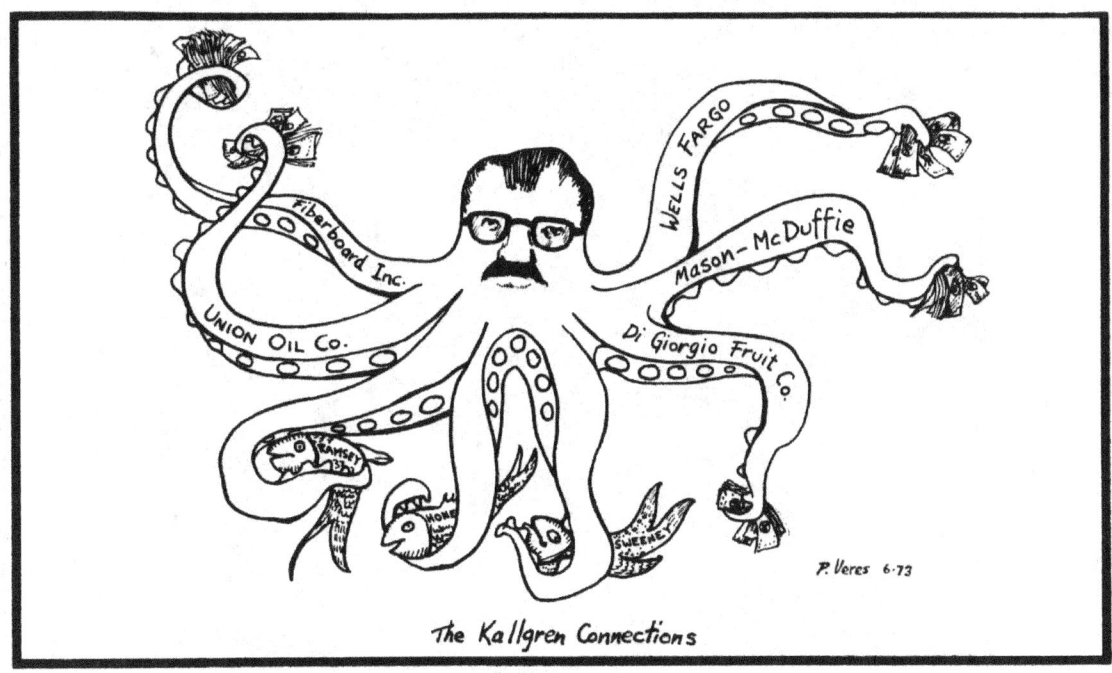

The Kallgren Connections

FAST EDDIE : KALLGREN THE HUSTLER

"I, Edward E. Kallgren, hereby declare that ... my present occupation is attorney."

—Statements of Candidates for Office, Berkeley Municipal Election, April, 1971

In April, 1971, Edward E. Kallgren was elected to the Berkeley City Council as the highest vote-getter in a field of 30 candidates. He ran on a platform of "ability, effectiveness, and integrity."

Two years later he would be the chief architect of the "Berkeley 4" slate of candidates for city council, put together one night in his living room. During the course of the campaign he would work overtime rounding up money and votes for his slate and throw $1,000 of his own into the campaign chest. In two years Ed Kallgren had risen from a virtual unknown amongst the Berkeley populace, to the top of the power structure in Berkeley.

This rather remarkable rise to a position of political prominence would ostensibly appear quite inexplicable. One searches in vain through Kallgren's public career in Berkeley or his record on the City Council for some reason, some key to his success. In vain because the key to understanding Kallgren's power lies not in Berkeley, but across the bay in a suite of offices deep in the heart of San Francisco's financial district.

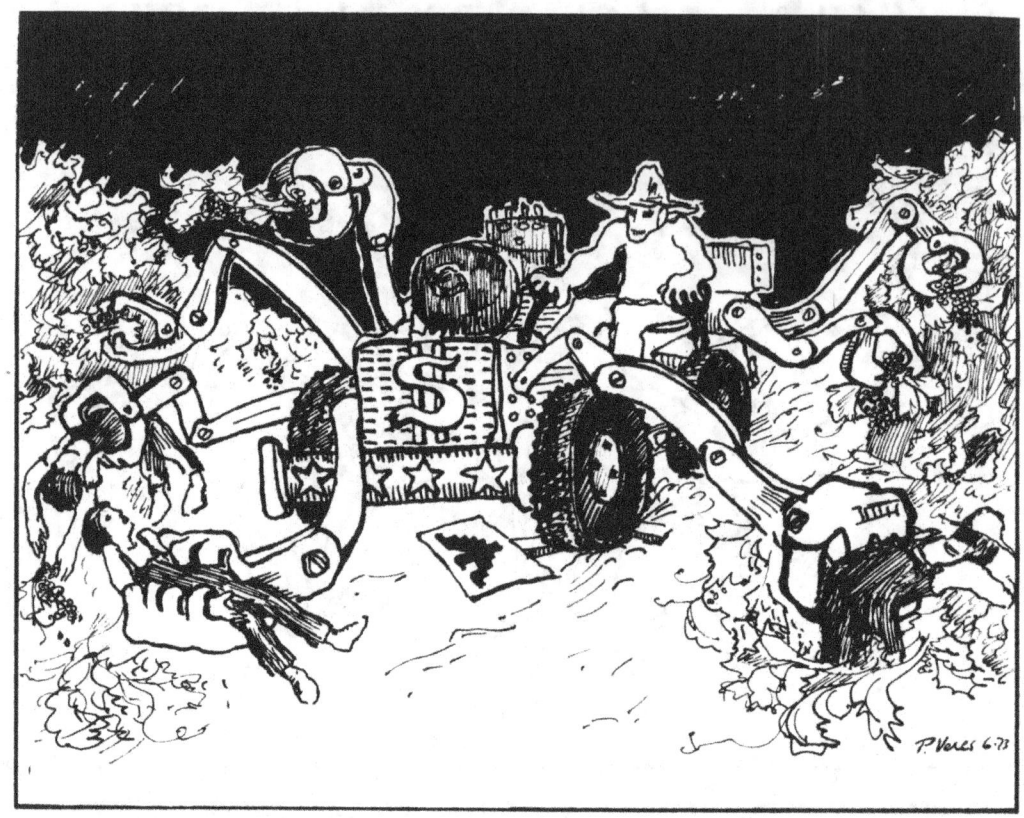

SOUR GRAPES

Agricultural scientists at U.C. Davis have developed a mechanical grape harvester, threatening a large number of jobs in California vineyards. So far they have found that only certain varieties of wine grapes can be harvested directly with the "vibratory machines." Because of excessive fruit damage, mechanical harvesting of raisin grapes requires extra labor. After raisin grapes ripen, farm workers sever fruiting canes allowing the grapes to partially dry on the vine. Partially dried fruit is less susceptible to bruising and subsequent decay.

Although the U.C. scientists have observed profoundly that "cane severance is a relatively simple concept..." other words, over half the farmworkers now doing this job will have to look elsewhere for work.

But there is one satisfaction for farm workers and friends of farm workers and ex-farm workers. The powerful pneumatic shears easily cut through trellis wire. The scientists find that "any cutting of the trellis wire is undesirable since the severed wire sags to the ground and the fruit cannot be detached by the harvester. In some cases, this may result in the complete loss of the fruit... and the cost of trellis maintenance is increased. (But) the use of a high tensile strength cane wire may provide a practical solution to this problem..."

Part of the article about the problems with grape harvest mechanization. The drawing depicts a kind of agribusiness Grim Reaper.

Vol. II, No. 1 July, 1973

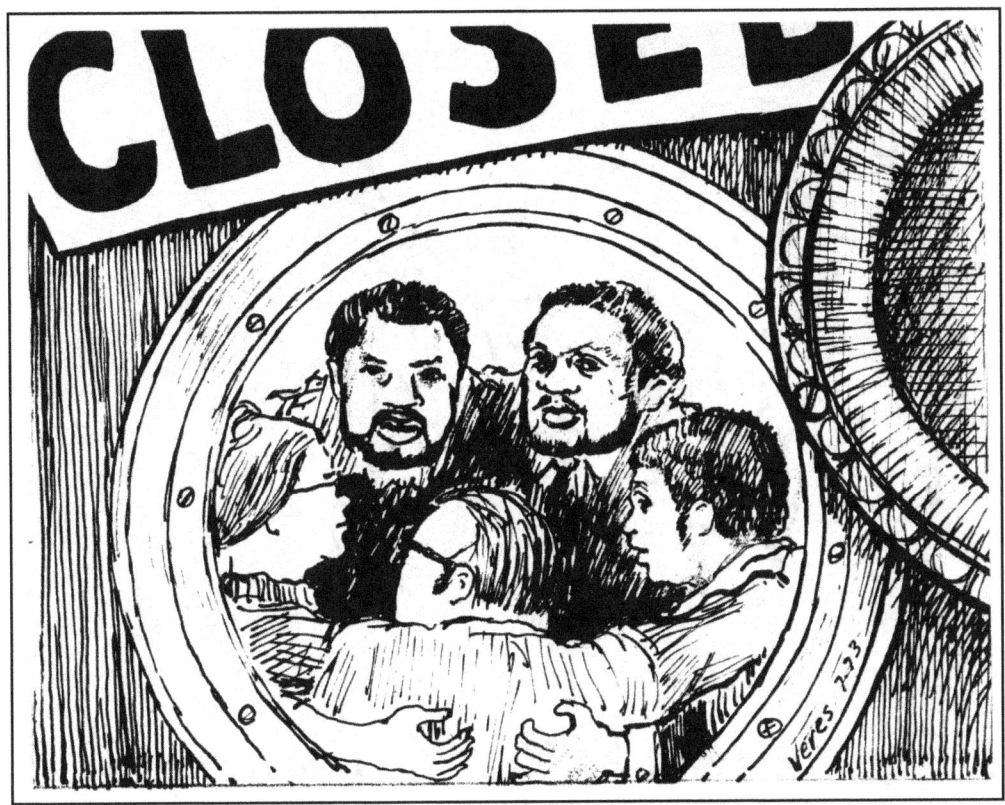

COUNCIL COUPS

Since taking office several months ago, the "liberal" council majority has taken the first steps toward keeping the workings of city government a secret from the people of Berkeley. Under the guise of "getting things done," the Berkeley Five have carried council meetings into the small hours of the morning, long after most working people have gone to bed, and past the time when KPFB has gone off the air. The only source of immediate information of council doings for the majority of Berkeley citizens is the Richmond-based *Gazette* (a publication so lacking in credibility that even the Bailey Recall Committee refuses to acknowledge it as a bona fide Berkeley paper). If the "liberals" want to "get things done," they shouldn't do it at the expense of the public's right to know. They should hold meetings every night if necessary, but end them at a reasonable hour.

The Berkeley Five's penchant for moving meetings to secret "executive sessions" whenever they don't want to let the people see what they're doing is another example of their attitude towards the public's right to know. This denial of such a basic right forces Berkeley citizens to rely on the necessarily-biased accounts of one side or the other. Why are the liberals afraid to let us see for ourselves what goes on behind those closed doors?

From the left: Sue Hone, Wilmont Sweeney, Henry Ramsey, Warren Widener, Ed Kallgren.

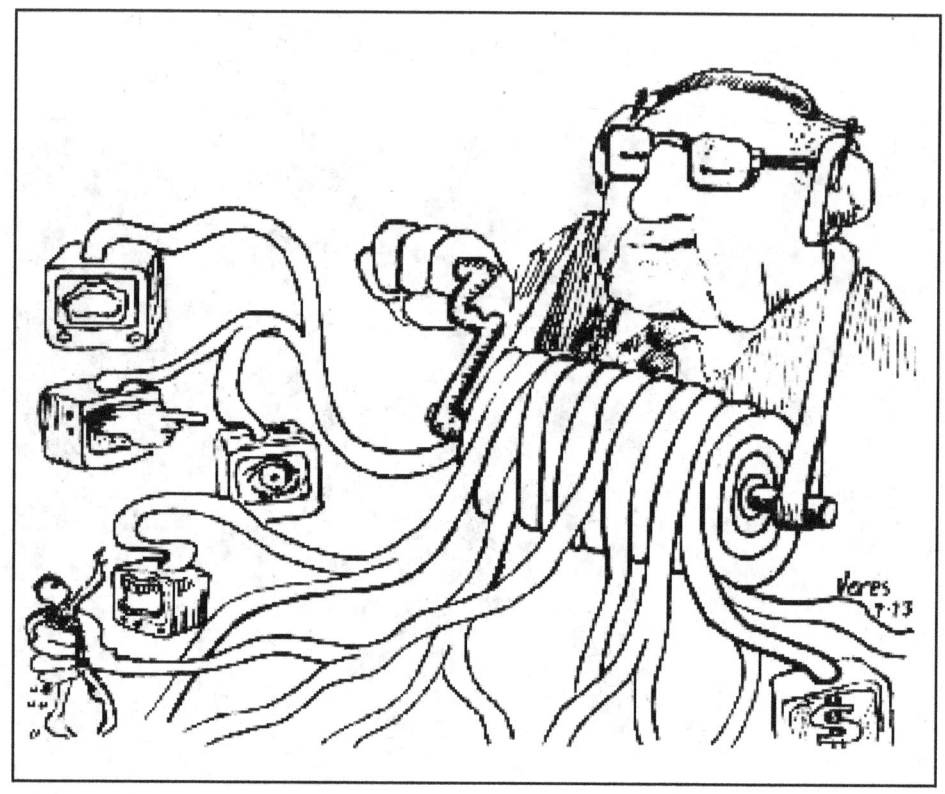

CITY CABLE TV POTENTIAL LOST

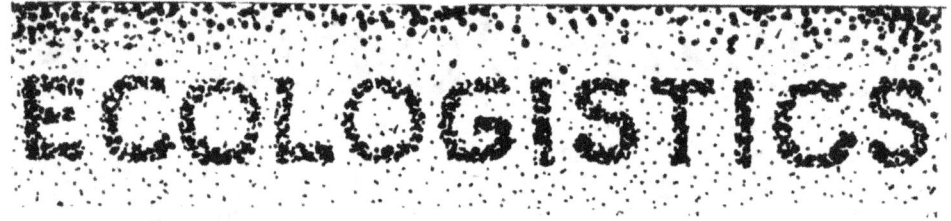

A logo for a column on product safety and environmental protection issues.

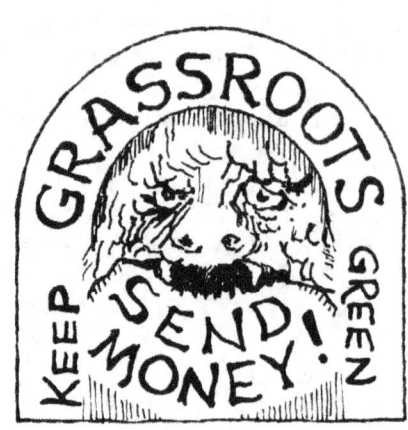

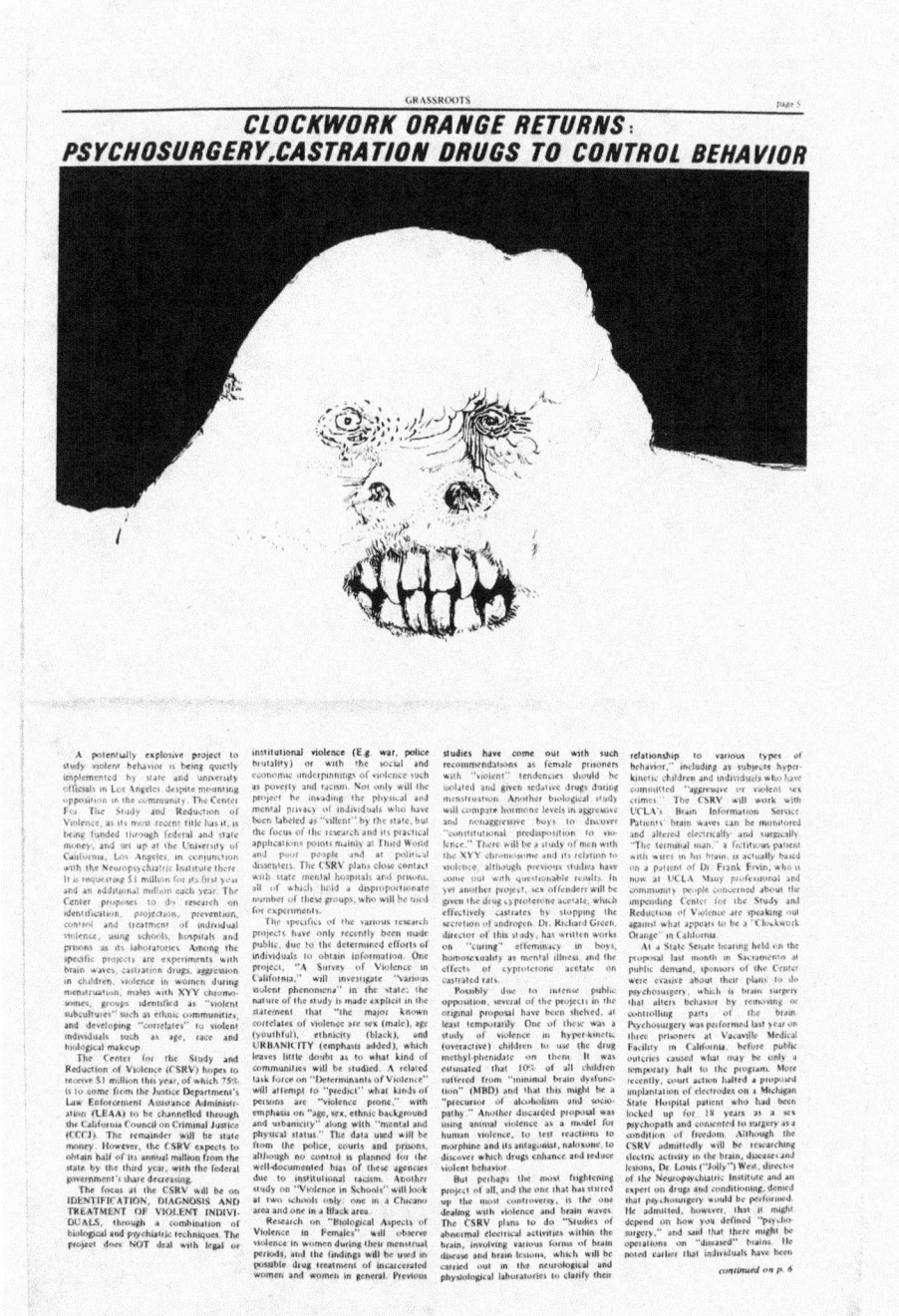

CLOCKWORK ORANGE RETURNS : PSYCHOSURGERY, CASTRATION DRUGS TO CONTROL BEHAVIOR

This is the fist page of a long article on a project in Los Angeles by The Center for the Study of Violence, to study violent behavior funded through federal and state money. As the headline indicates, this is not a benign prospect for society, and there was intense public opposition to the projects being proposed. My drawings reflect the fear factor in the proposals.

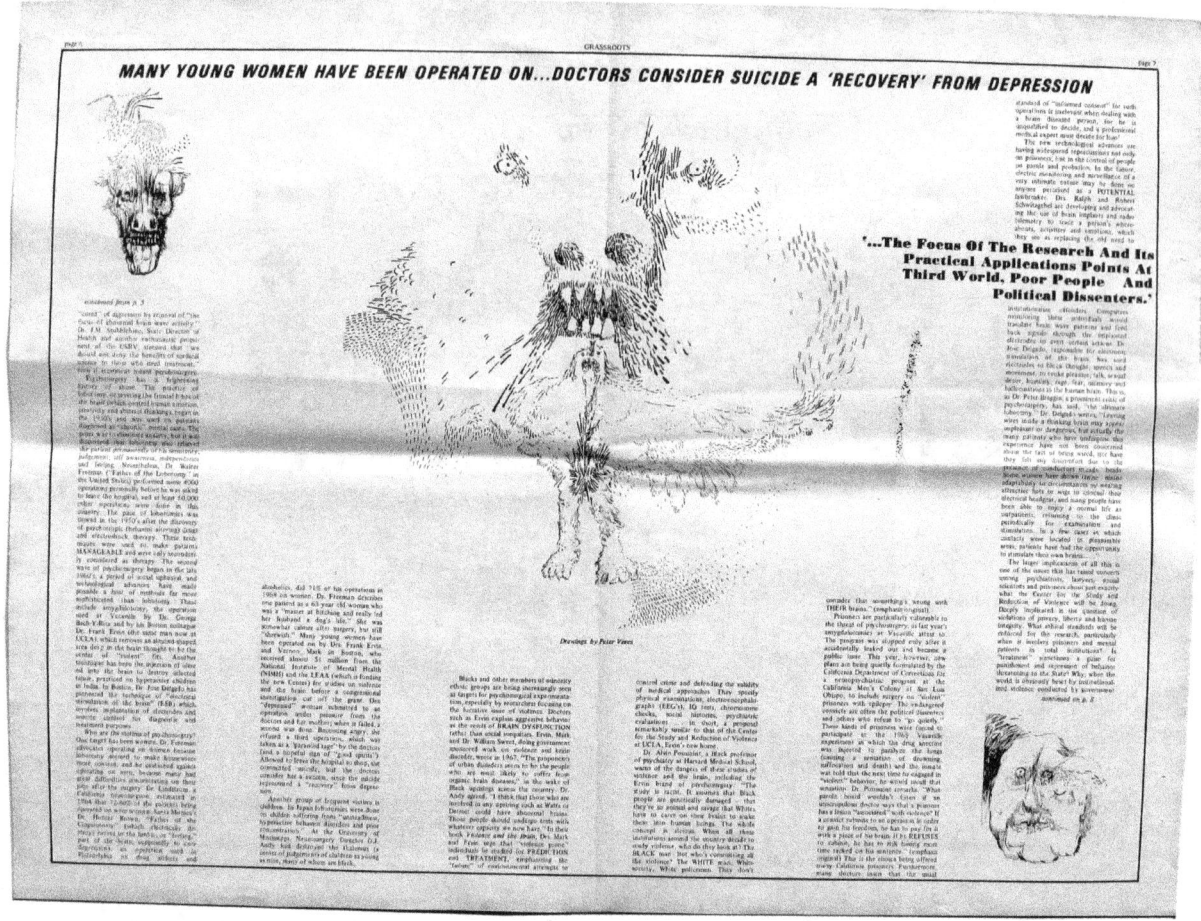

In illustrating this article I used the kinds of images I was making outside of Grassroots.

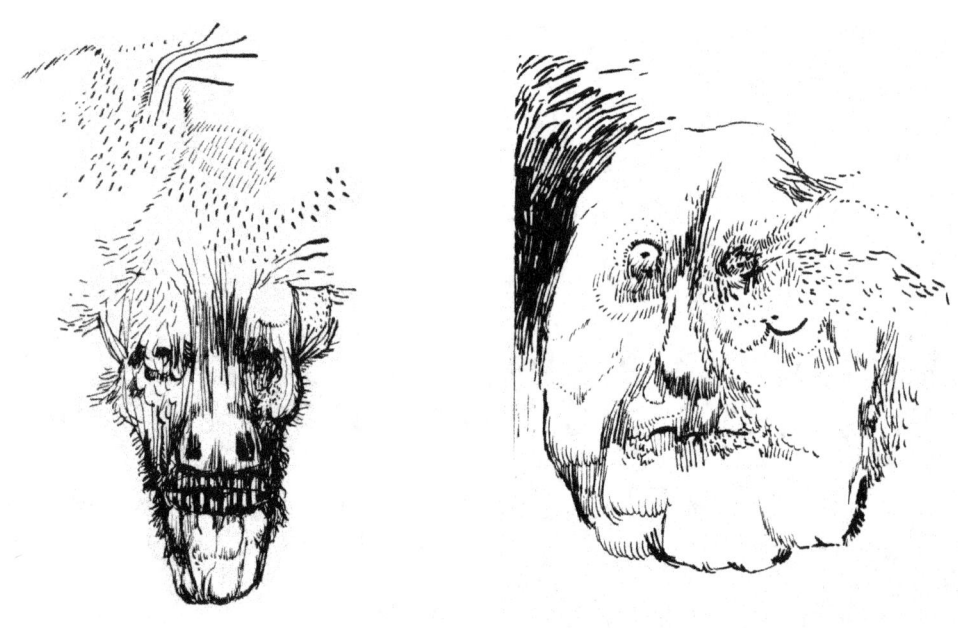

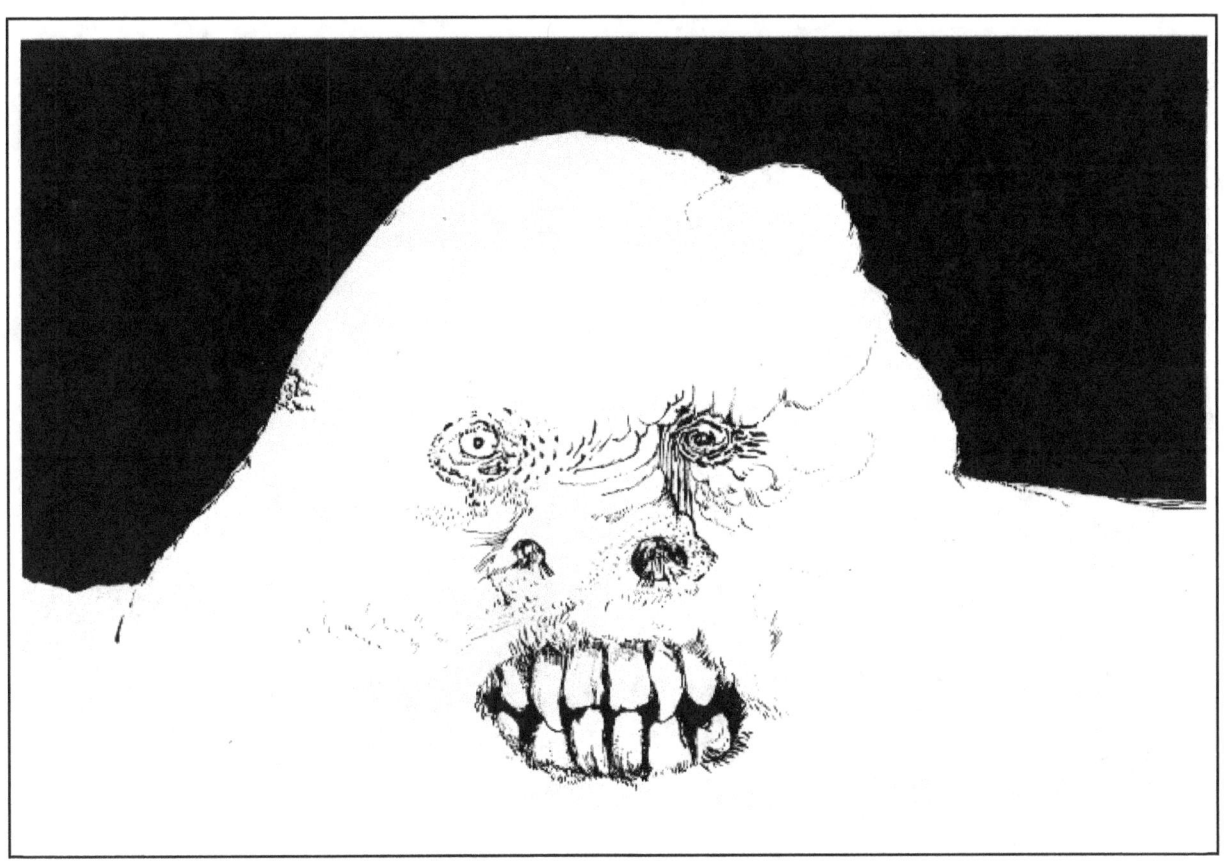

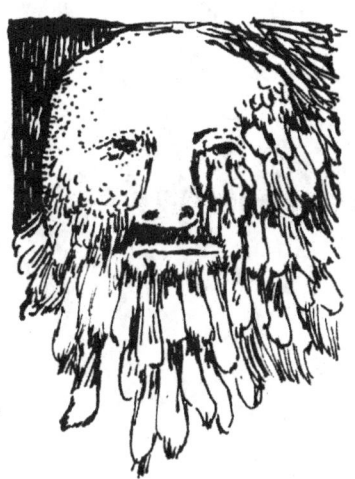

the man who wished for feathers ~

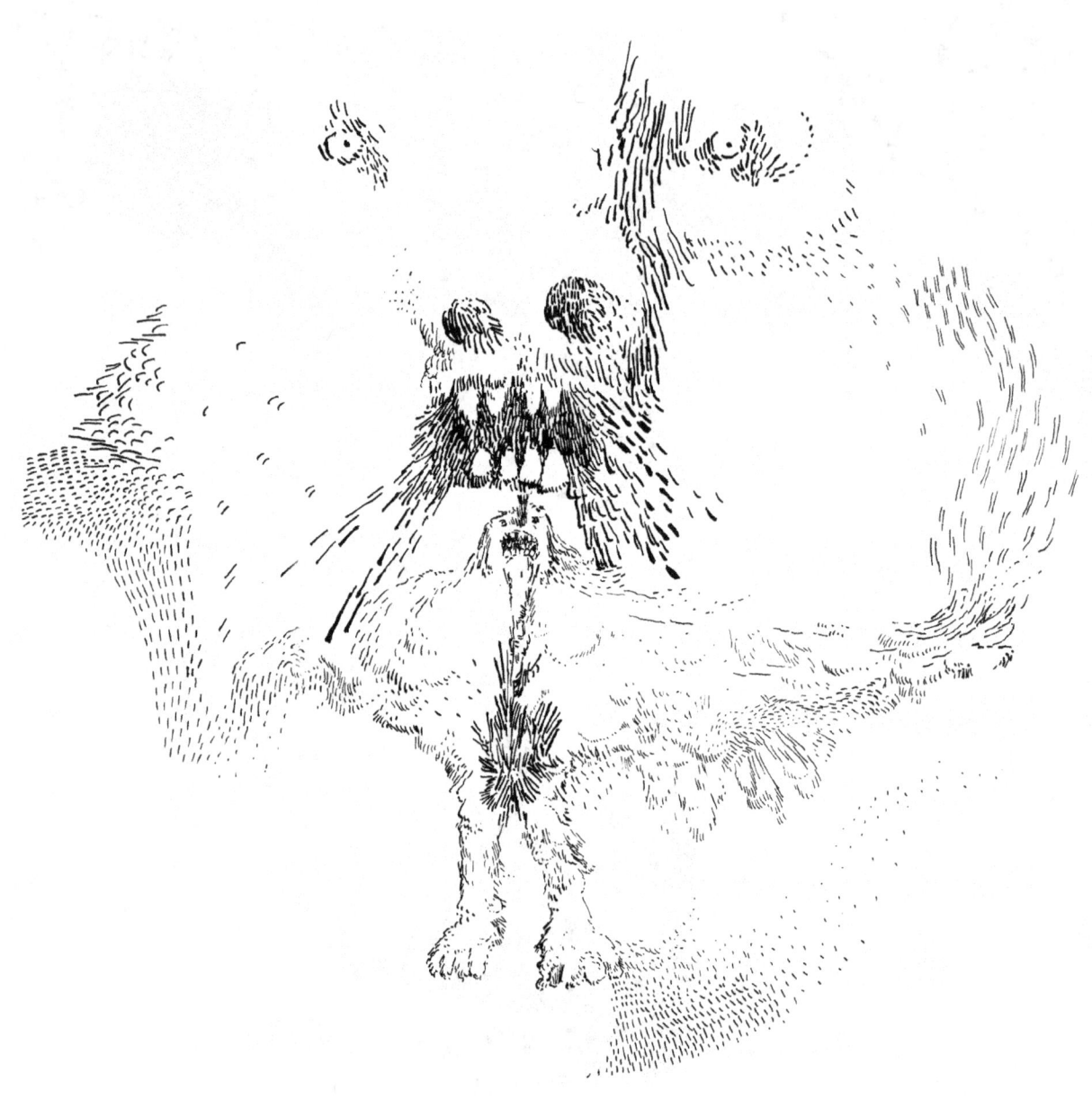

Vol. II, No.3 September 12–October 2, 1973

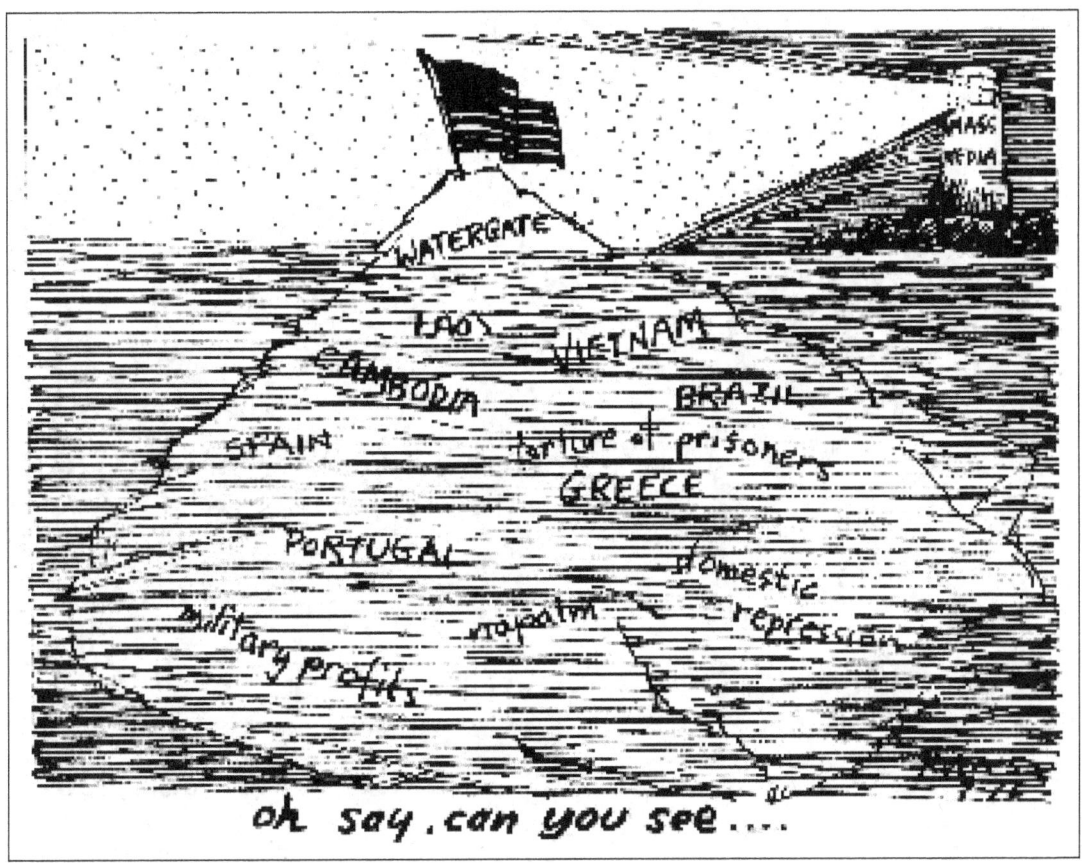

Not an image for an article, this editorial drawing was just a comment on what the news media were focusing on. And on what they were ignoring – the treacherous mass under the visible ice.

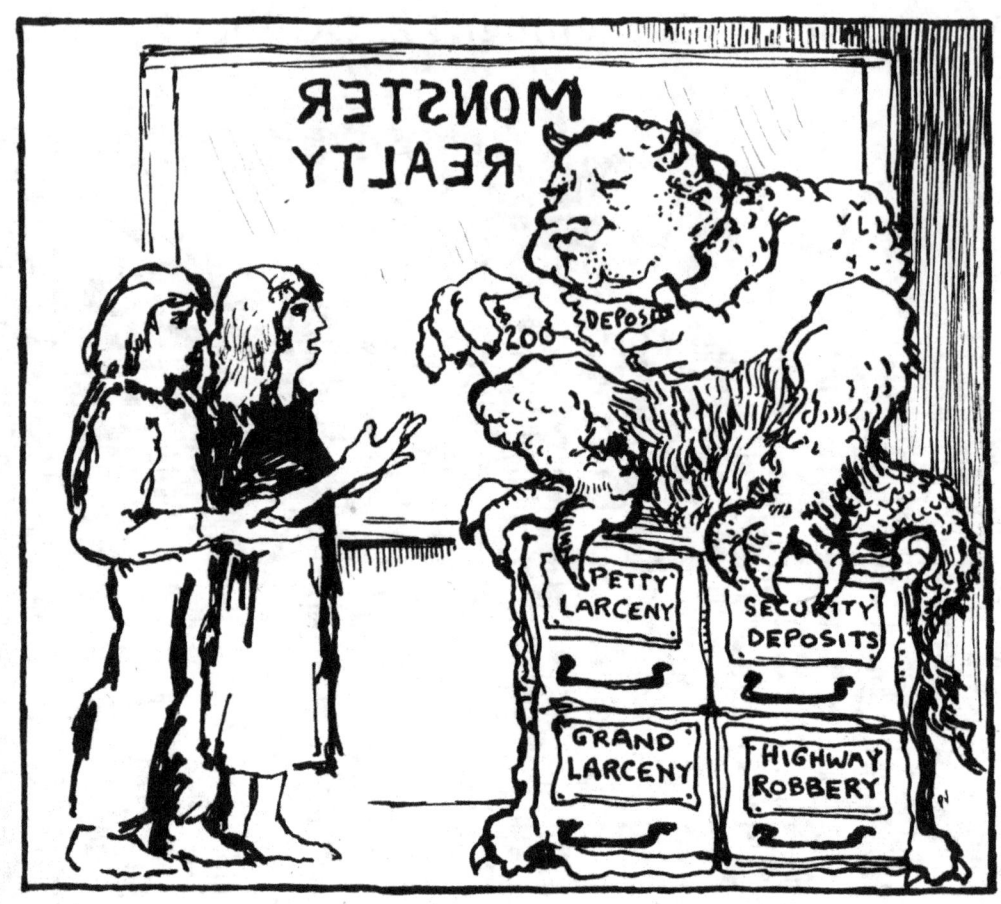

TENANTS TAKE NOTE: GET YOUR MONEY BACK

An article on the many ways some landlords rip off tenants.

Vol. II, No.4 October 3–16, 1973

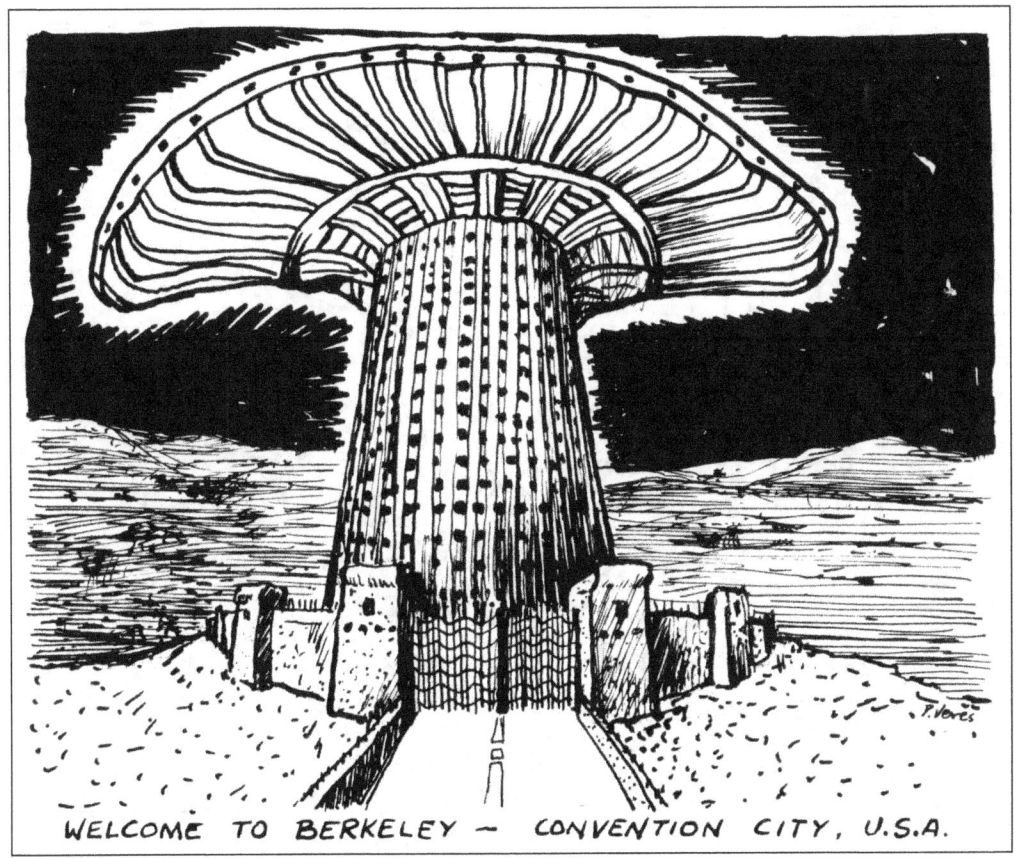

WELCOME TO BERKELEY — CONVENTION CITY, U.S.A.

$500,000 GAMBLE

The Berkeley City Council will within the next few weeks have before it a proposed *Cooperation Agreement* between HUD and the City of Berkeley. This agreement commits the City to put up $500,000 by November 1st of this year if the Berkeley Redevelopment Agency (BRA) has not sold a note to finance the West Berkeley Industrial Park.

The City Council has not for many months dealt with any of the issues that surround this project. A growing number of independent studies point to its probable failure.

The Council has not officially reviewed the 1½-year-old Payne-Maxie report (for which it paid $5,000), or the recent HUD Environmental Impact Study. A state-required environmental impact study is due soon. Now it is proposed to gamble $500,000 on an unpopular project, lacking public confidence for several years. This half-million will follow five million of federal and local money to tear down five homes, widen four blocks of a street, empty many other sound residential structures (forcing their occupants to compete for Berkeley's scarce housing, or leave town); all in the name of an

Vol. II, No. 5   October 17–November 6, 1973

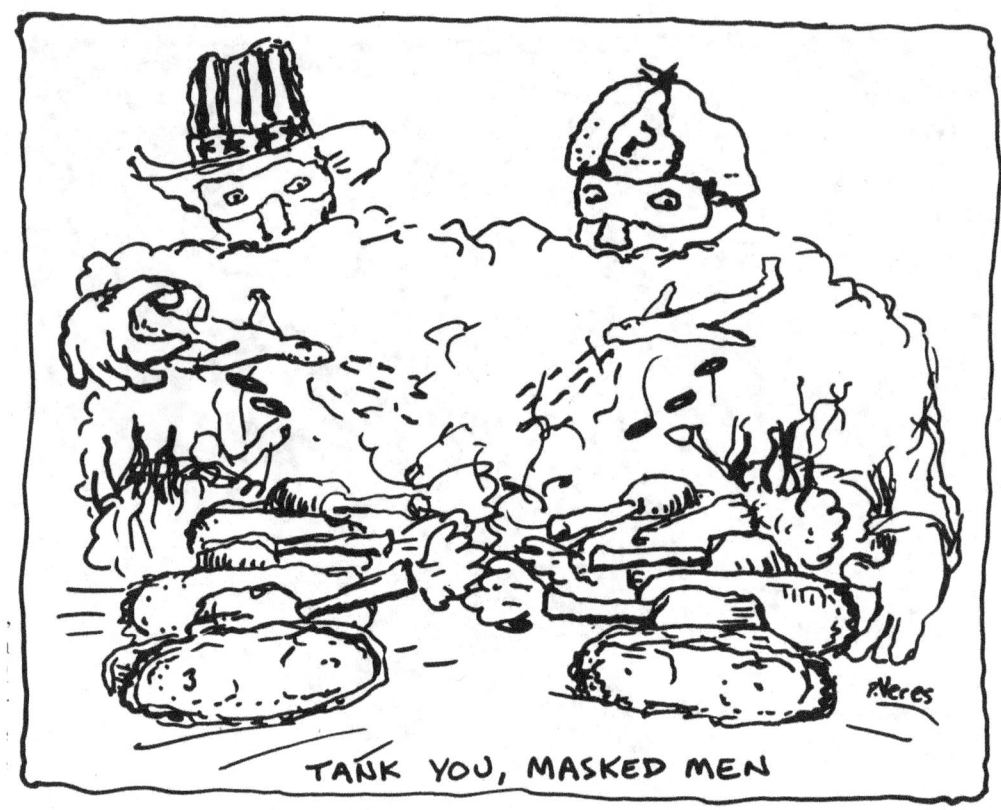

Though this drawing was on the editorial page there was no article about bombs or tanks, or Americans and Russians. So I don't know why I drew this except that the two big powers were at it as usual. There was a Lenny Bruce routine, "Thank you Mask Man", dealing with The Lone Ranger, which was made into a funny animation. I twisted the title into the drawing's caption.

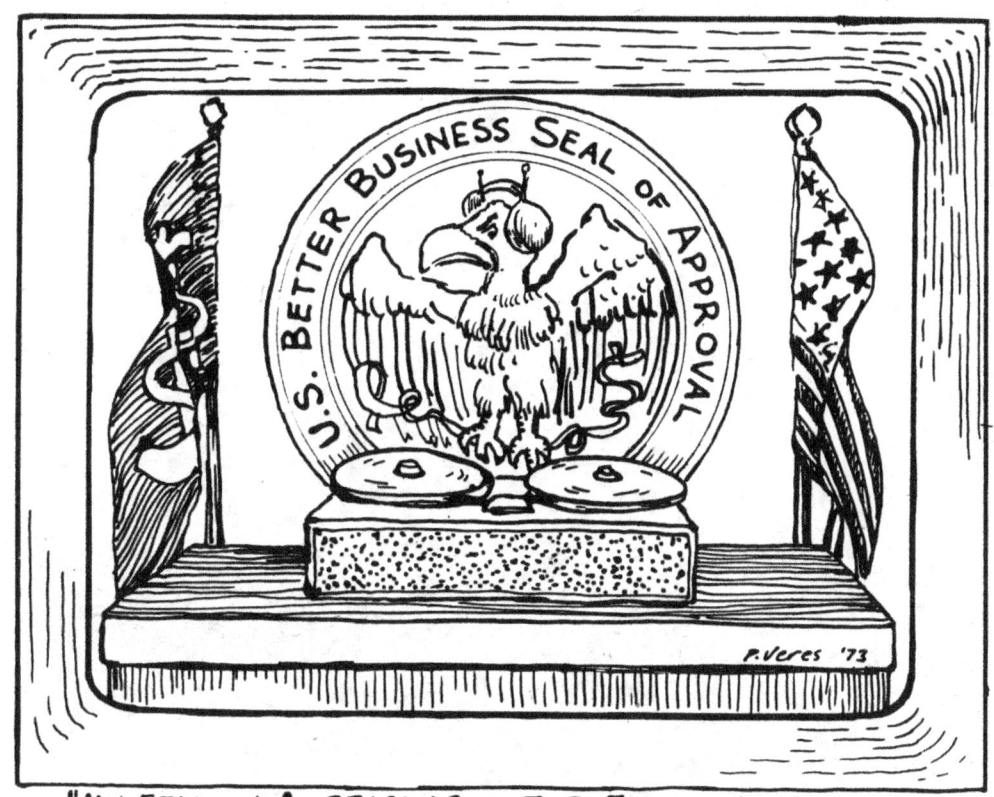

"MY FELLOW AMERICANS... THE FOLLOWING OFFICIAL LIES HAVE BEEN PRE-RECORDED..."

This again is a cartoon with no story attached, and does not address a local issue. But the story of the missing 18 minutes of Nixon's secretly recorded White House tapes was very much in the news and I decided to have a shot at it. The eagle with the headphones is holding some tape in its talons in the seal behind the tape recorder. Today, in 2012, a reel-to-reel tape recorder is an unknown relic of another century, so the drawing may be undecipherable by the digital generation.

Vol. II, No. 7   November 21–December 4, 1973

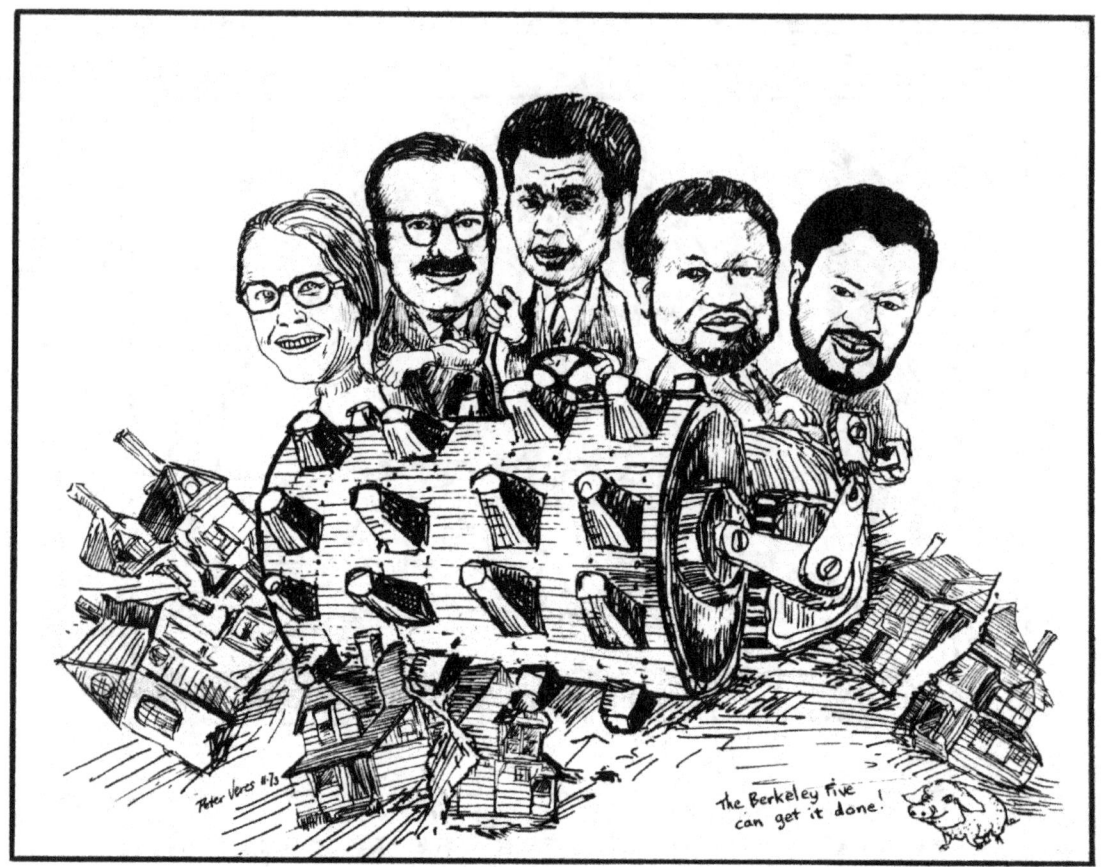

The nominally liberal majority of the City Council, the Berkeley Five – Sue Hone, Ed Kallgren, Mayor Widener, Wilmont Sweeney, Henry Ramsey – were pushing to bulldoze the West Berkeley Ocean View neighborhood to make way for the plans of the Berkeley Redevelopment Agency and the West Berkeley Industrial Park. The little pig says: The Berkeley Five can get it done!

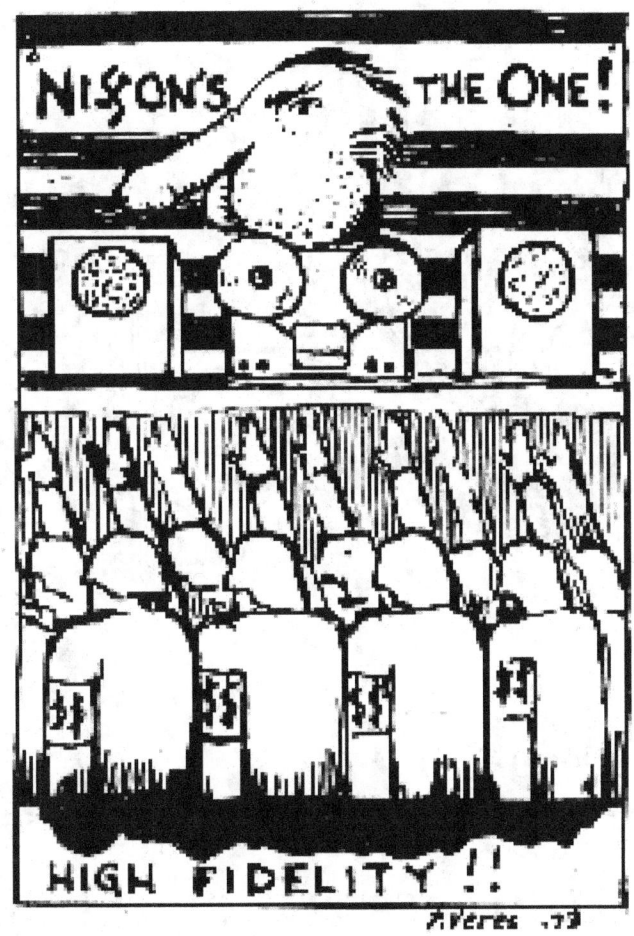

Another Nixon cartoon: Tricky Dick, the X turned to a swastika, his tape recordings, the flag's stripes, and helmeted troops wearing their $$ armbands saluting the Chief. Super subtle over all.

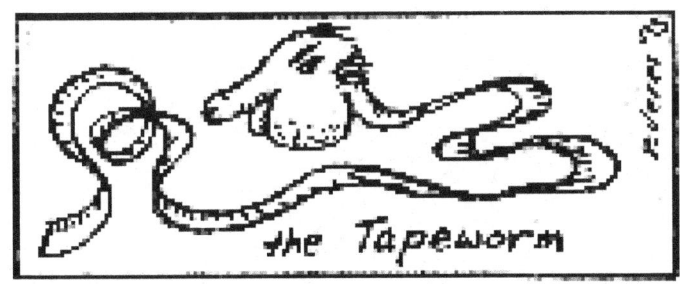

A small space-filler on the same theme, in the previous issue.

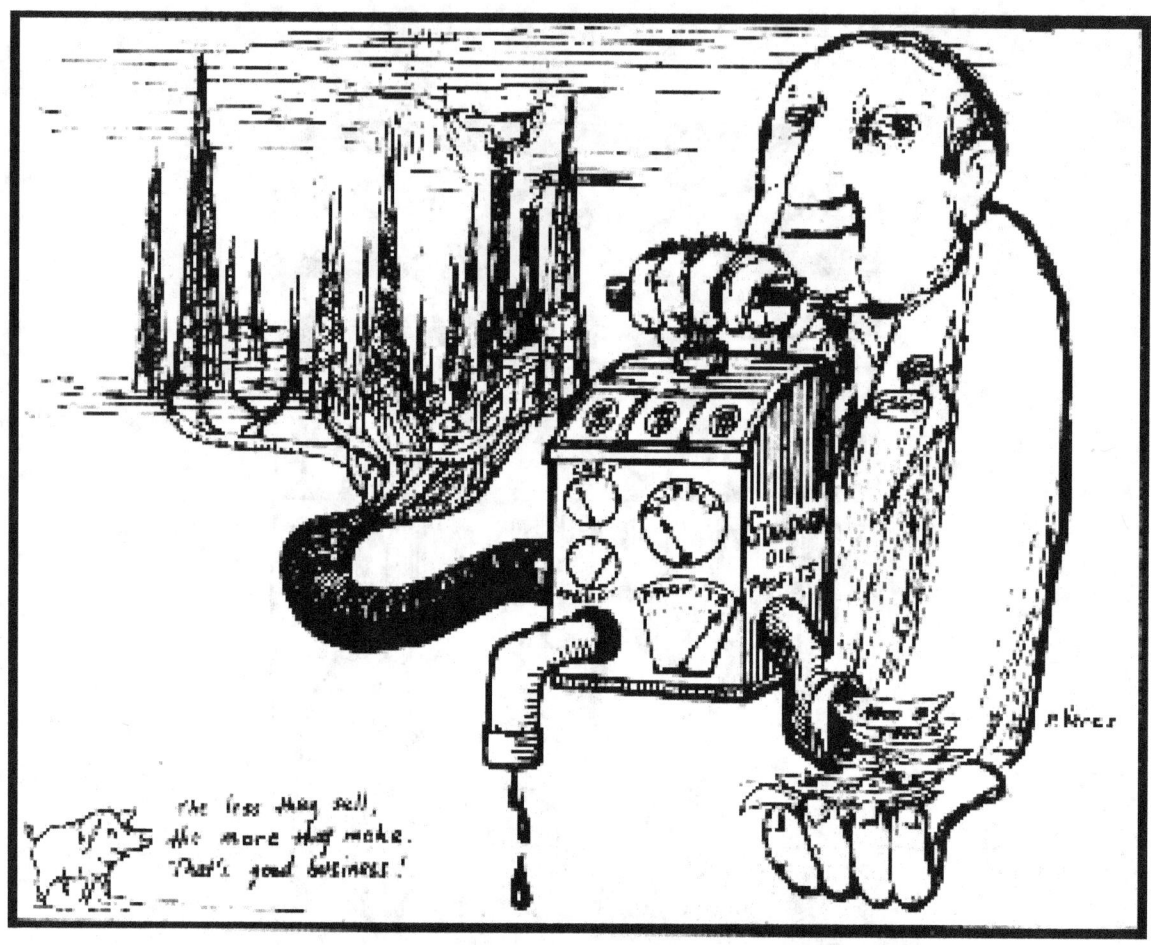

DELLUMS REPORTS ON ENERGY

A long report by Congressman Ron Dellums on the Nixon Administration's energy policies. Of course they were supporting the big energy players. The labels read Cost, Supply, Subsidy and Profits. Cost and Supply are low, Subsidy and Profits high. There's no business like oil business.

The little pig says: The less they sell the more they make. That's good business!

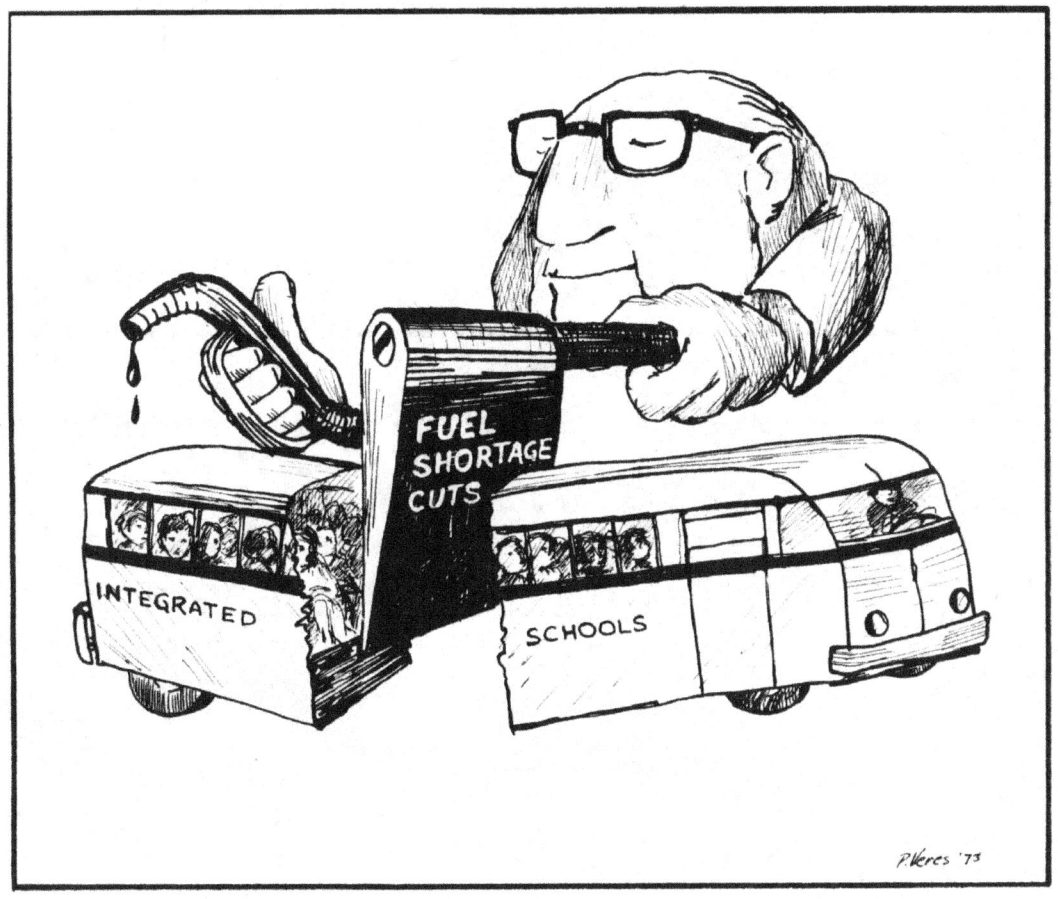

SCHOOL BOARD – BUSING SLOWED?

> **DON'T REVERSE INTEGRATION**
> Board President Mary Jane Johnson noted, "In tonight's paper a Democrat from Virginia wanted to tack onto the fuel bill the buses used for integration. ... I don't want the "energy crisis" to be the vehicle to reverse the gains we have made. I want every step taken to ensure that kids continue to go to school and that buses bring children together. I have very little faith in Washington."
> Stoll added that "The late bus is critical" in bringing kids together for after school activities.

A section from the article.

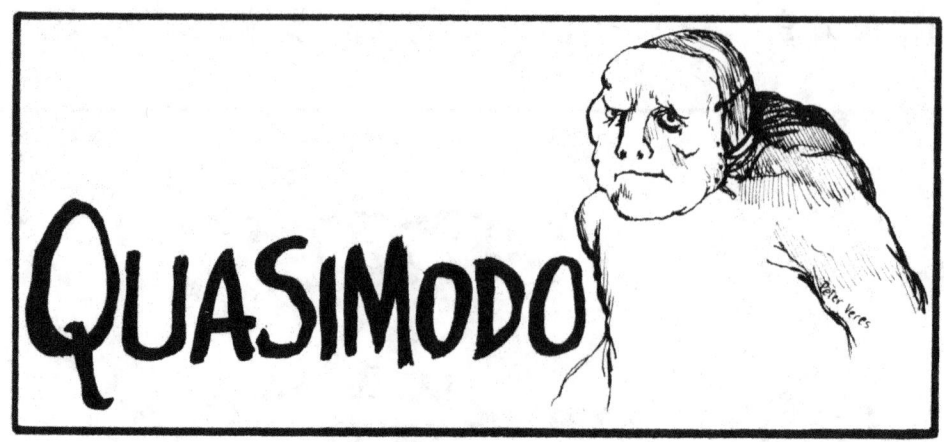

This was a very personal, well-written column about the disabled community. I didn't know who the writer was in real life, just that Quasimodo was his nom de plume, so in addition to the hump I gave him a mask. He finally revealed himself as Michael Williams in the October 2-15, 1974 issue, Vol.3, No. 7. In that logo I added his real name under Quasimodo.

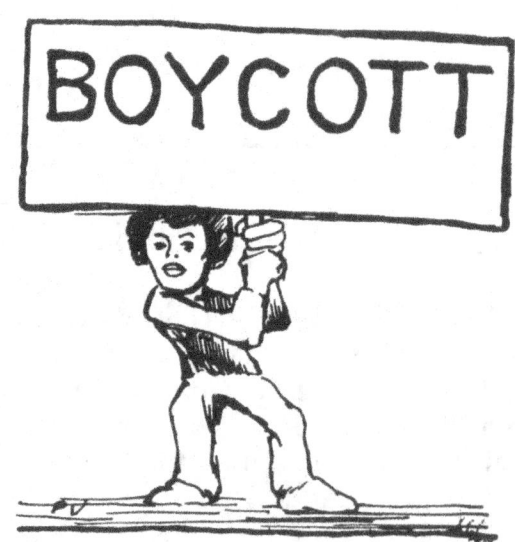

Below this drawing was a long list of firms which were, at that time, on the "We Don't Patronize" list of the California Labor Federation, AFL-CIO. The list, headed by Coors Beer, included many movie theaters, restaurants, and Sears stores.

Vol. II, No. 14   March 5-18, 1974

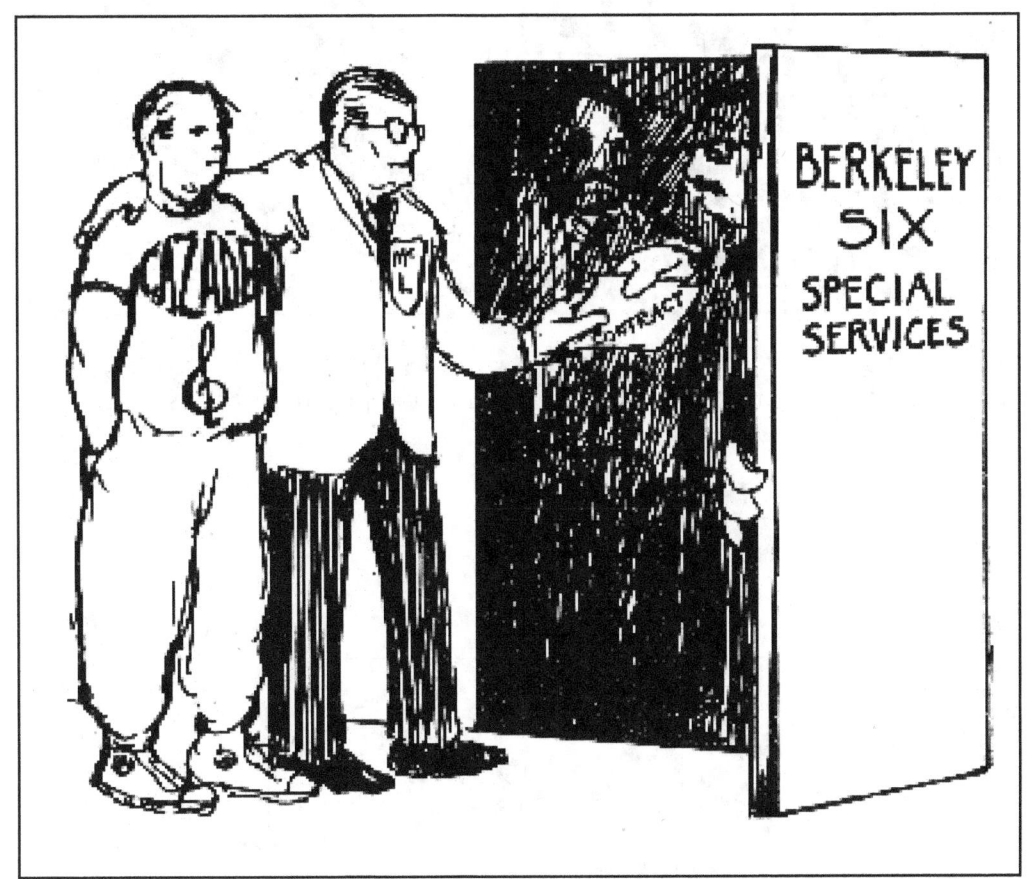

CAZADERO PAYOLA – A PIECE FOR SIX PLAYERS

> On February 19, the same Berkeley Six that could not afford $9,000 for city playground supervision, voted for a four-year contract for Robert Lutt, Director of Cazadero Summer Music Camp. Lutt's annual pay from the city jumped from $5,000 to $17,750. Not a bad raise, even for times of runaway inflation.

This is the lead paragraph of a long article about the politics behind this deal. Councilman McLaren apparently had a "long personal involvement with Lutt", the guy on the left shown as a camp coach with a Cazadera shirt.

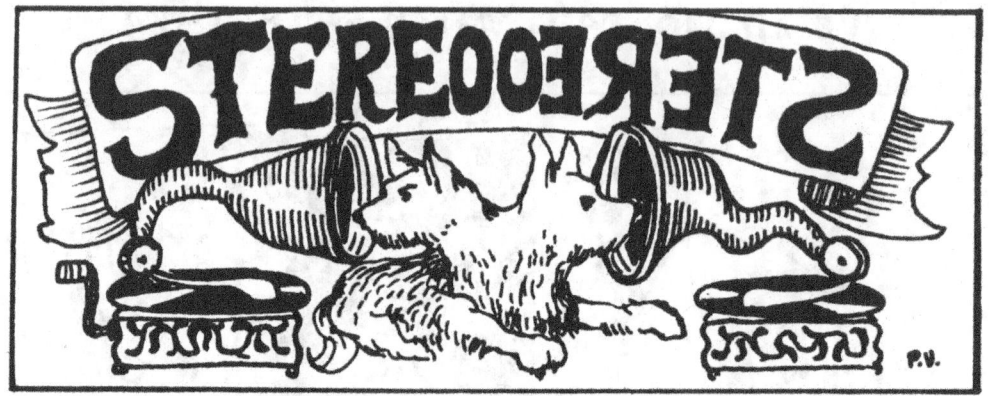

Despite my drawing's reference to the old RCA His Master's Voice logo, this was not a column about music or records but about stereo music equipment by a stereo repairman.

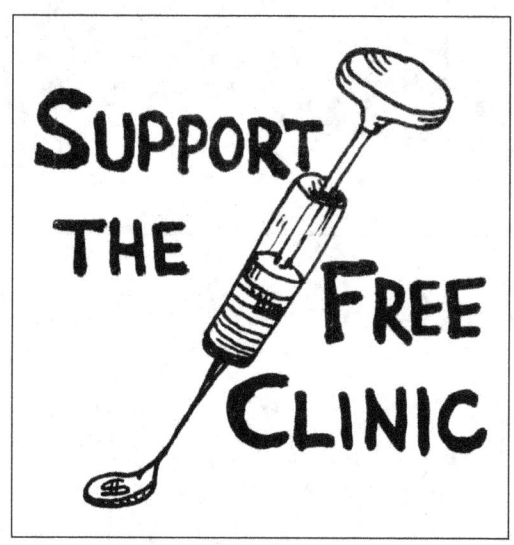

CHANGES AT THE FREE CLINIC

A report on the evolution and the ongoing work of the Berkeley Free Clinic.

Vol. II, No. 15   March 20–April 2, 1974

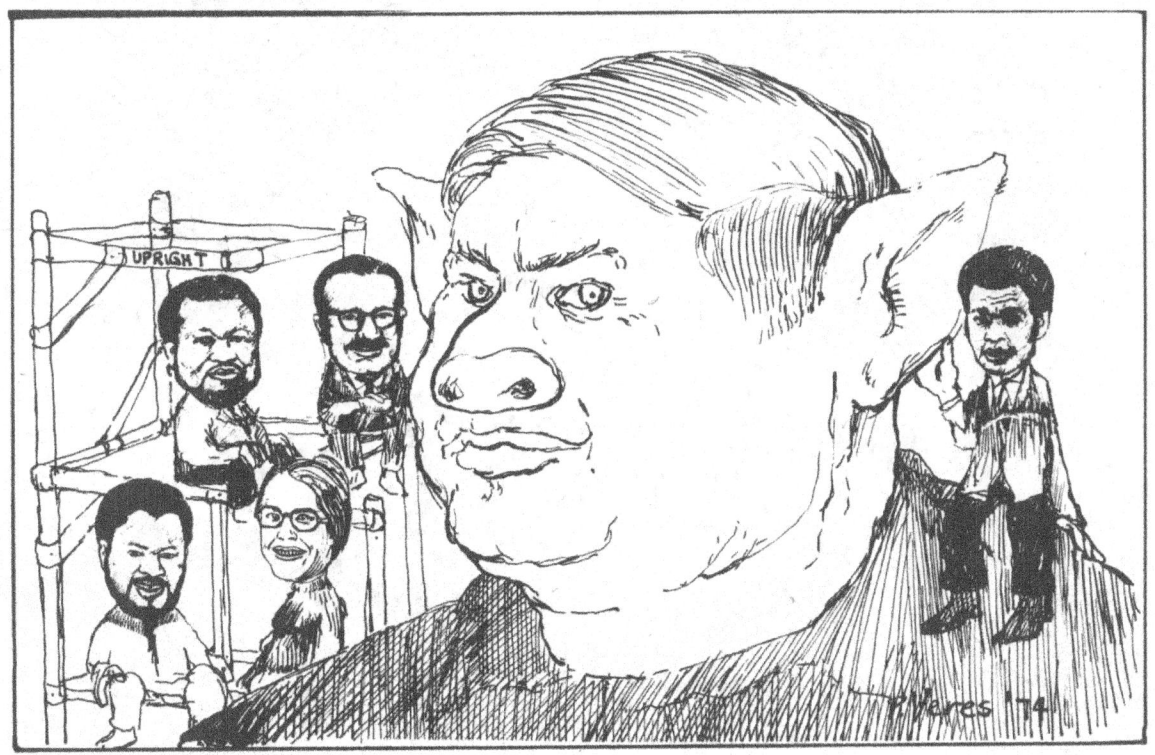

CAN WE TRUST TAYLOR?

John Taylor, Berkeley's City Manager, was discussed in the editorial. Surrounding him are the Berkeley Five. The scaffolding on the left is marked UPRIGHT on the top crossbar – UpRight was a Berkeley company, a manufacturer of scaffolds. Founder and owner Wallace Johnson was a former Republican Mayor of Berkeley, who supported conservative politics and politicians in Berkeley.

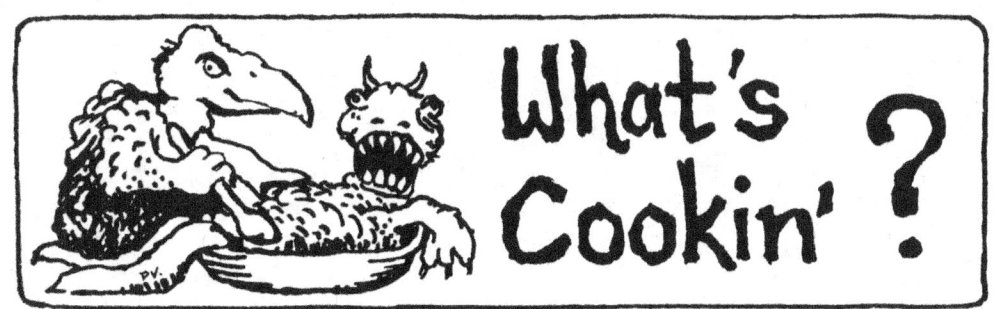

A food column, of course, with recipes.

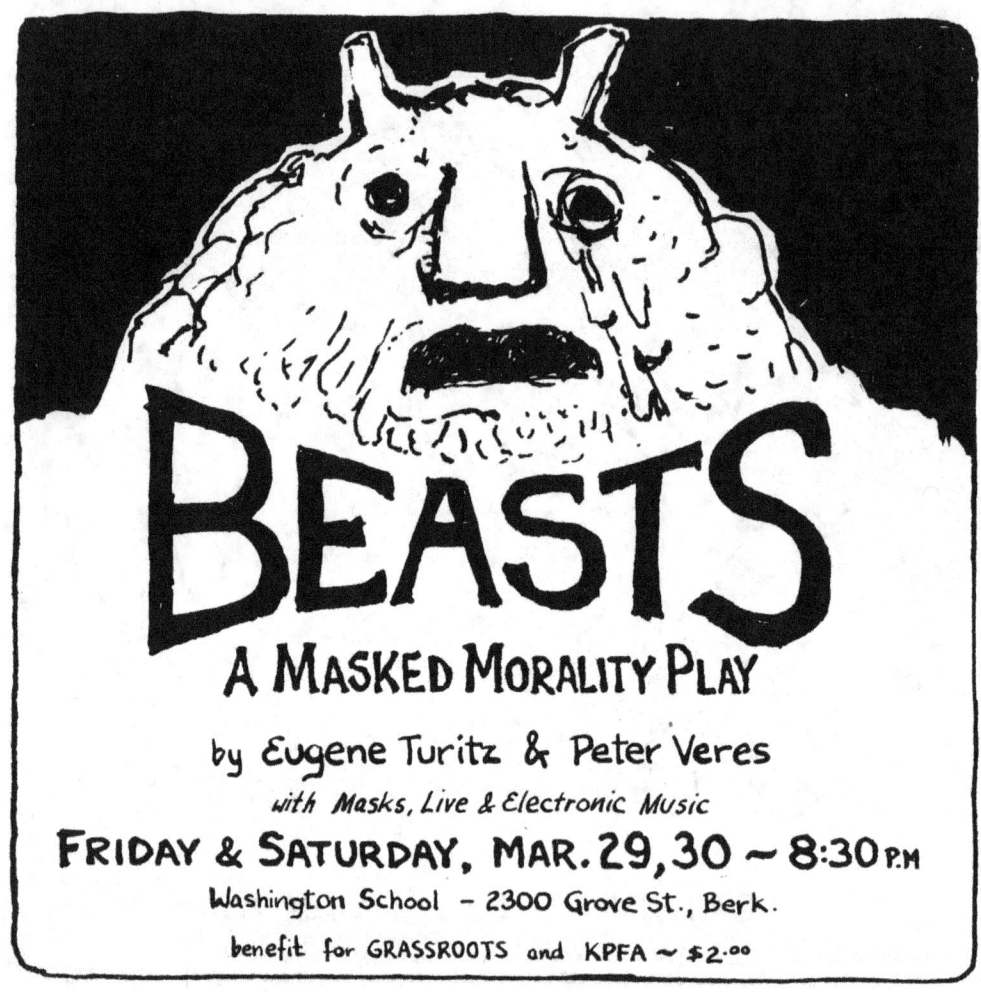

One of several ads announcing our performance piece, BEASTS.

Vol. II, No. 17   April 24–May 7, 1974

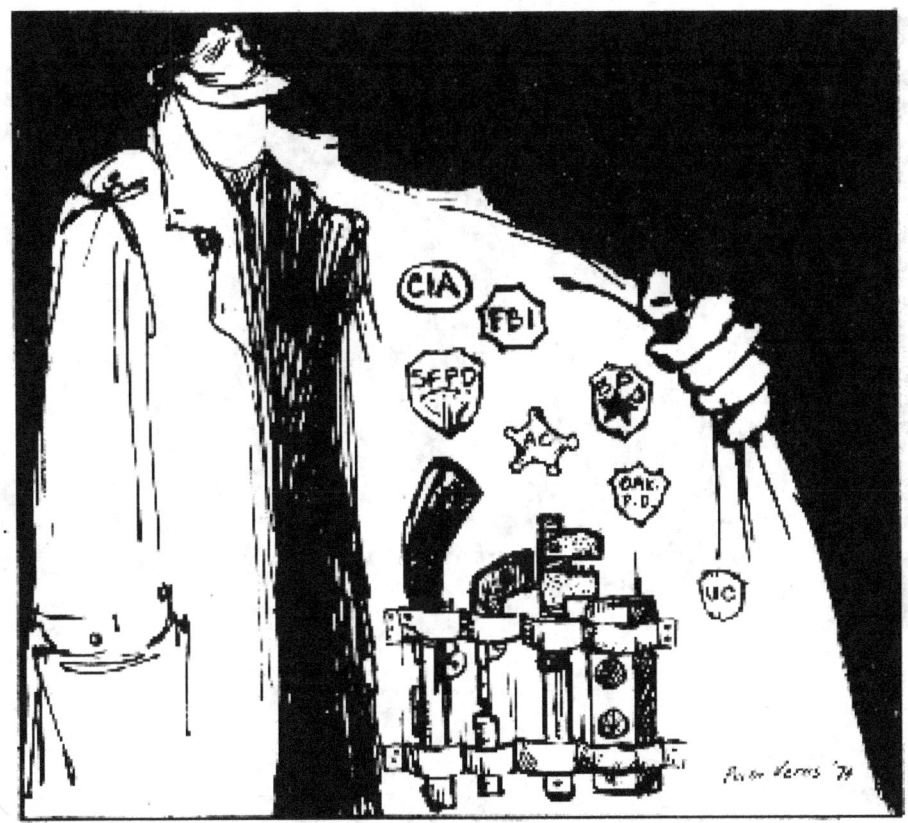

POLICE TERRORISM

When Mayor Alioto announced last week that he was using the Zebra slayings as a rationale for conducting a witch-hunt in the Black community, he was acting in concert with police throughout the area who have intensified their usual harassment of Blacks.

In Berkeley, almost simultaneous with Alioto's latest outrage, our police force instigated a raid, carried out with the Oakalnd Police Department, on the Black Panther Party headquarters. The raid was absurd, even by police standards. Working with a trumped-up warrant, they arrested 14 Party members and displayed an incredible arsenal of "confiscated" weapons one day, then dropped all charges the next. But that's not bad for a department which considers Charles Crane, the Inspector who last week shot an unarmed Black youth, "one of the most outstanding investigators in the country."

Above is the lead of the editorial. Alioto was Mayor of San Francisco, and the Zebra killings were of white victims by four black men, from October 1973 to April 1974. The drawing shows a faceless weapons dealer with badges which include besides the CIA and FBI the SF Police Dept., Berkeley P.D., Oakland P.D., Alameda County, and the University cops. To the left of the walkie-talkie is a wrench, a nod to Nixon's Watergate burglars known as the "Plumbers".

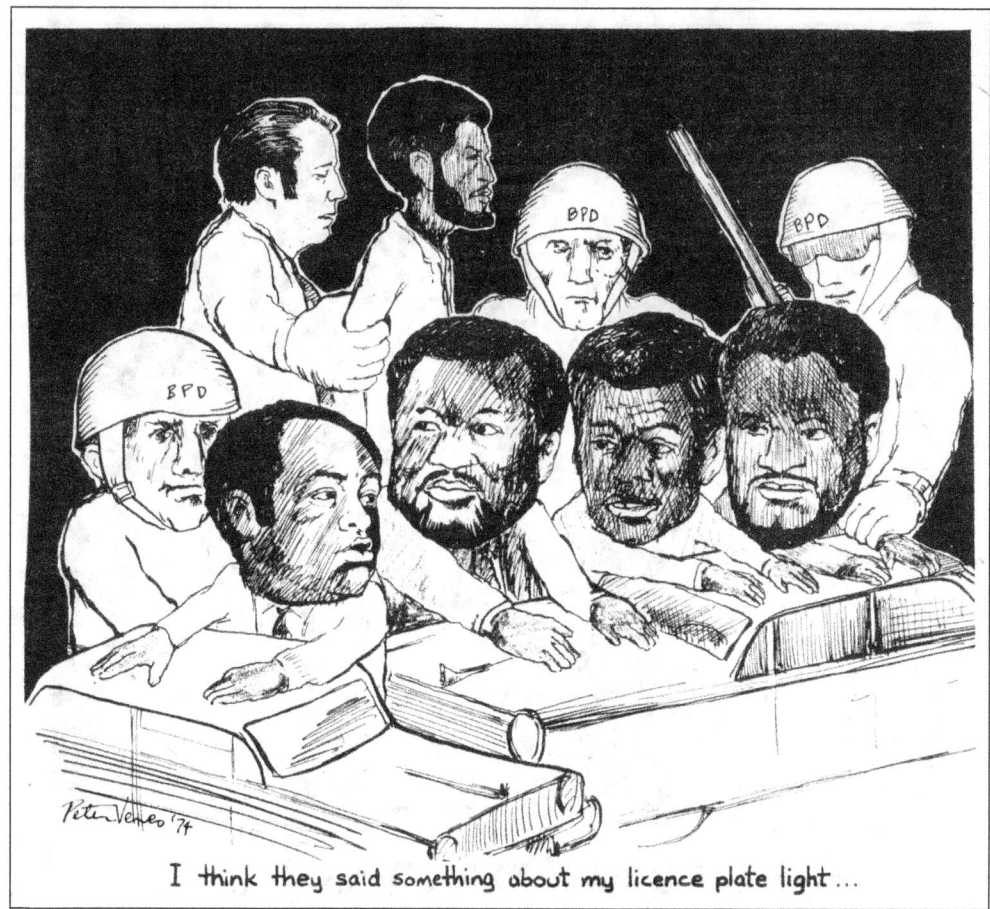

I think they said something about my licence plate light...

COUNCIL'S SURPRISING RESPONSE

The City Council's recent action against the police for their harassment of Blacks was as welcome as it was surprising. It's not often we see our "representatives" respond so readily to their constituency as they did in calling for the indictment of former police Inspector Charles Crane and demanding an end to the Zebra manhunt.

The Council acted at a critical time: the San Francisco police were involved in an unprecedented witch-hunt throughout the Black community, and Oakland and Berkeley police had just conducted a completely unjustified raid on Black Panther Party headquarters. It was also just one week after Crane shot an unarmed twelve-year old Black youth.

Whatever the reasons for this surprisingly progressive vote, we have to suspend our usual criticism of the Council long enough to congratulate that body for taking a strong stand against these outrageous police actions.

We also join the Council in commending City Manager John Taylor for his expeditious firing of Crane. We hope Taylor will continue to use the power of his office to end police racism and brutality. Crane should not simply be a scapegoat to defuse the issue. His firing and possible indictment are good precedents for the city to follow in future cases of police misconduct.

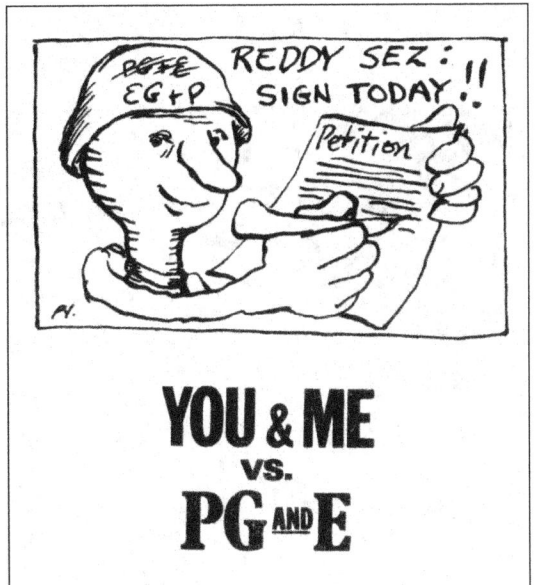

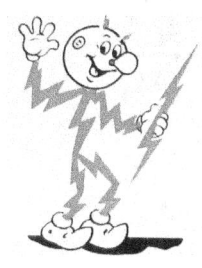

YOU AND ME AGAINST PG&E: NEW ACTION ON INITIATIVE

PG&E's advertising mascot was Reddy Kilowatt. EG&P stood for Electricity and Gas for the People. Below is part of the long article.

Last year, the people of Berkeley faced their first major battle with PG&E. In the most expensive political campaign in Berkeley history, PG&E and its corporate friends spent upwards of $100,000 to stop community ownership of Berkeley's electric system. But their propaganda, obfuscation and outright lies could not change the fact that the city's independent feasibility study concluded that "substantial long-term economic benefits would accrue to the people of the City of Berkeley if the city acquired and operated its own electric distribution system" and that early years of operation would net an average $500,000 per year.

"BATTLE OF BERKELEY"

However, on April 17, 1973, the latest battle of Berkeley was lost to PG&E by a 58 to 42 percent vote. In celebration, PG&E rewarded the people of Berkeley with repeated massive rate increases and requests that will raise average monthly bills more than 50% by the end of this year.

Vol. II, No. 19   May 23–June 4, 1974

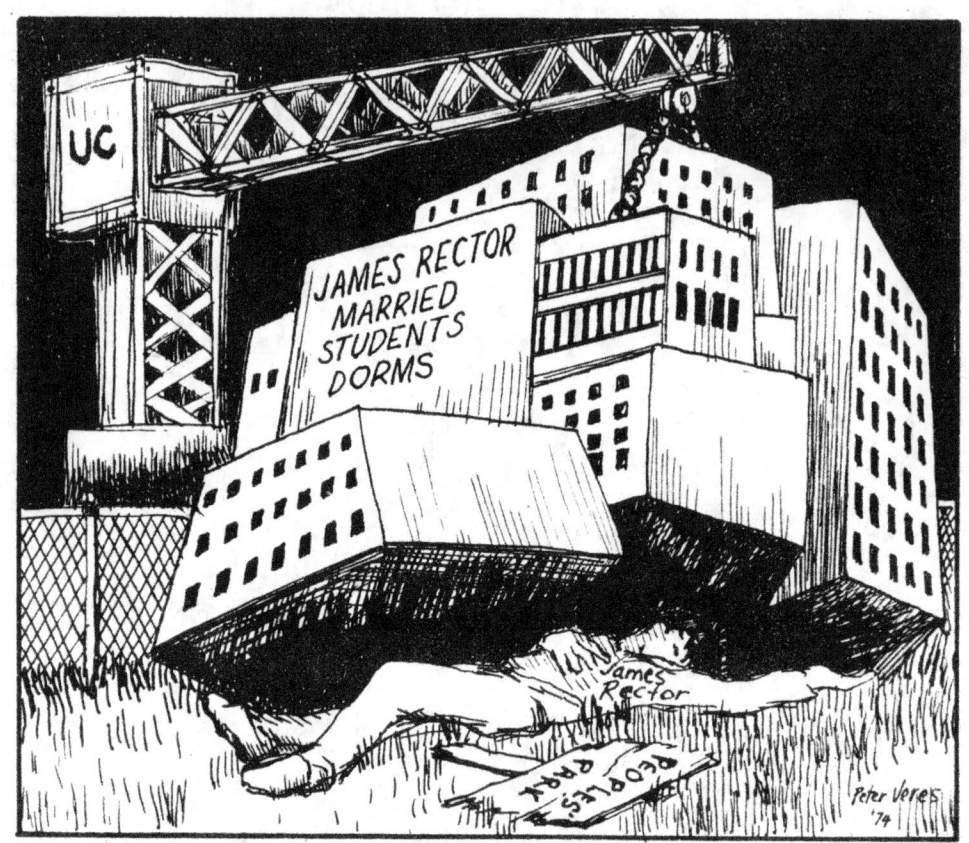

FORUM ON PEOPLES' PARK

This May month — which marks the fifth anniversary of the bloody battles for Peoples' Park — the University of California and the City-University Community Affairs Committee are soliciting Berkeley citizens' opinions on how the park site should be used and/or developed.

Tuesday, May 28, at 7:30 p.m. in

JAMES RECTOR HOUSING PROJECT

The University has seriously proposed that housing on Peoples' Park be named after James Rector, who was killed by police buckshot during the 1969 demonstrations at the Park. This should be considered "as a way of mitigating the negative impact which would result in loss of the symbolic value of the present site," according to the preliminary environmental impact study for the development.

Vol. II, No. 20   June 5–19, 1974

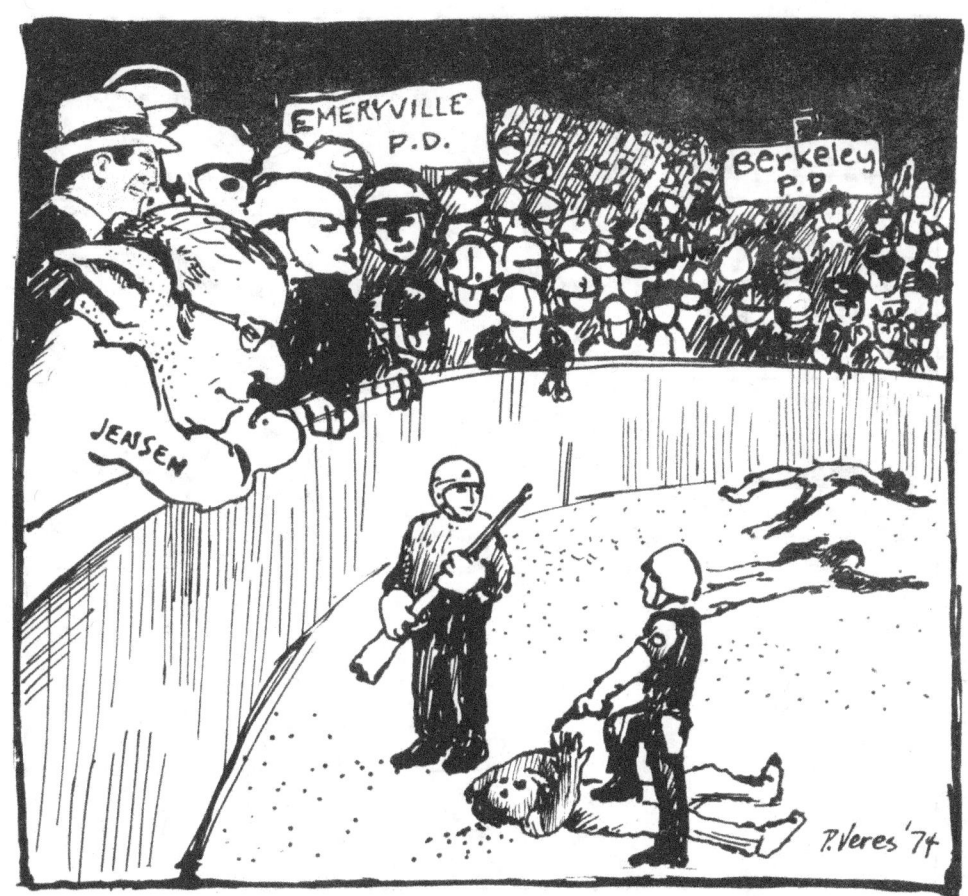

CRIME IN D.A.'S OFFICE

Our local police must be delighted with District Attorney Lowell Jensen's refusal last week to indict B.P.D. Inspector Charles Crane for shooting an unarmed black 12-year-old. Not only does it get a fellow officer off the hook, it also reaffirms Jensen's previous indication — that is, his refusal to prosecute the police officers who murdered 14-year-old Tyrone Guyton in Emeryville — that it is open season on Black youth. Any racist cop — and there are a few around — is now assured that he can blow away a Black son whenever he feels the urge, and do so with complete impunity.

The reasoning behind this blatant subversion of justice is incredible: "Crane violated no state law," says Jensen. Of course anybody else who started throwing lead around would be on ice before he could load a second string, but the police, claims the D.A., are above the law. City Manager John Taylor did well to fire Crane, but this outrage cries out for stronger stuff. Crane's act was a crime. He should stand trial.

The Berkeley City Council did well too. A majority voted to urge Jensen to indict. "We never got the letter," says the D.A.'s office, most certainly a lie. And while we're on the subject, how did that vote go? Rumford, a cop, abstained. Sweeney and Ramsey voted no. (So did Hone, but what do you expect?). We wonder, do they have sons?

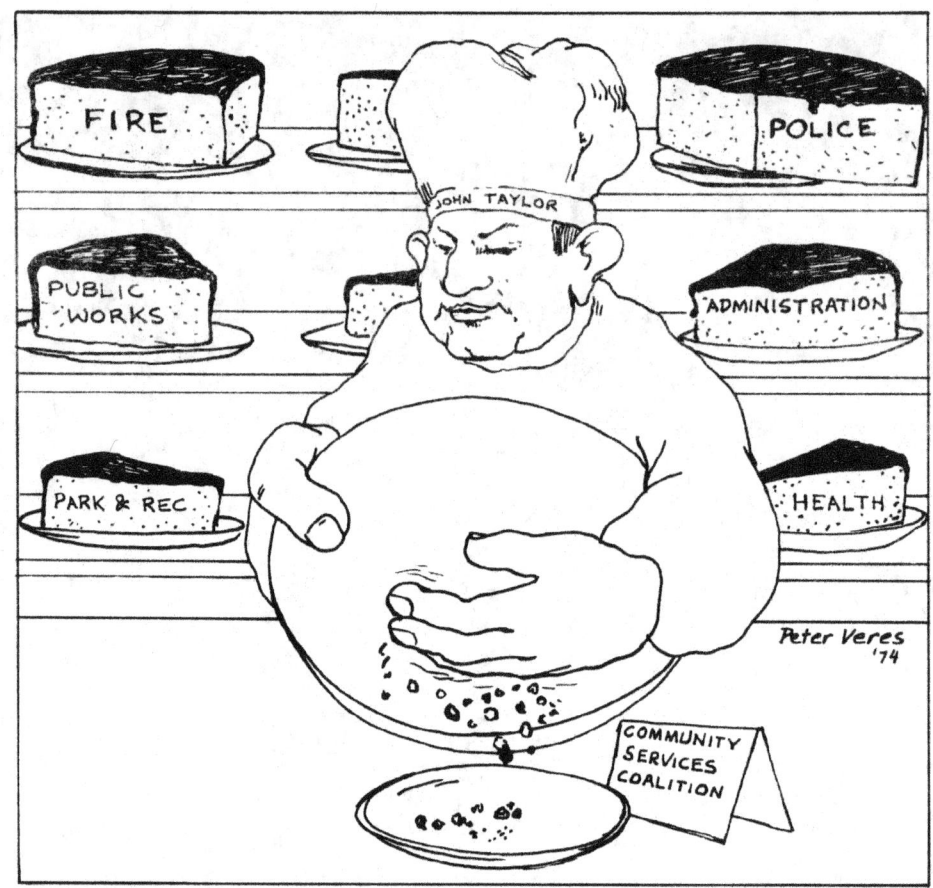

City Manager John Taylor doling out crumbs to the Community Services Coalition.

A WARM WELCOME TO SERVICES COALITION

The formation of the Community Services Coalition represents an exciting new development on the Berkeley political scene. Community agencies which provide direct, vitally necessary services to the people of Berkeley, are saying to the city: no more playing political games with our agencies. They have pulled together a coalition which won't allow the city council and county Board of Supervisors to play one group off against the other, and which demands tangible, not just verbal, recognition of their importance. GRASSROOTS fully supports their requests.

Their presentation at the Thursday, June 13, Council budget hearing was a beautiful one. While they expressed appreciation for the funding the city has provided in the past, they were strongly critical of the minimal amounts offered for this year. They had facts which strongly demonstrated how efficient they have been: as one example, the Women's Health Collective served 15,000 clients on a budget of $21,000. And there was no question about the logic on their side: the stirring presentation by Ed Roberts of the Center for Independent Living was just one highlight in an evening of forceful and irrefutable testimony.

Coalition representatives rightly said that it wasn't their job to figure out where the city can get the needed $1 million. The buck stops at the Council, and for the sake of a lot of people in Berkeley, they must come up with the money.

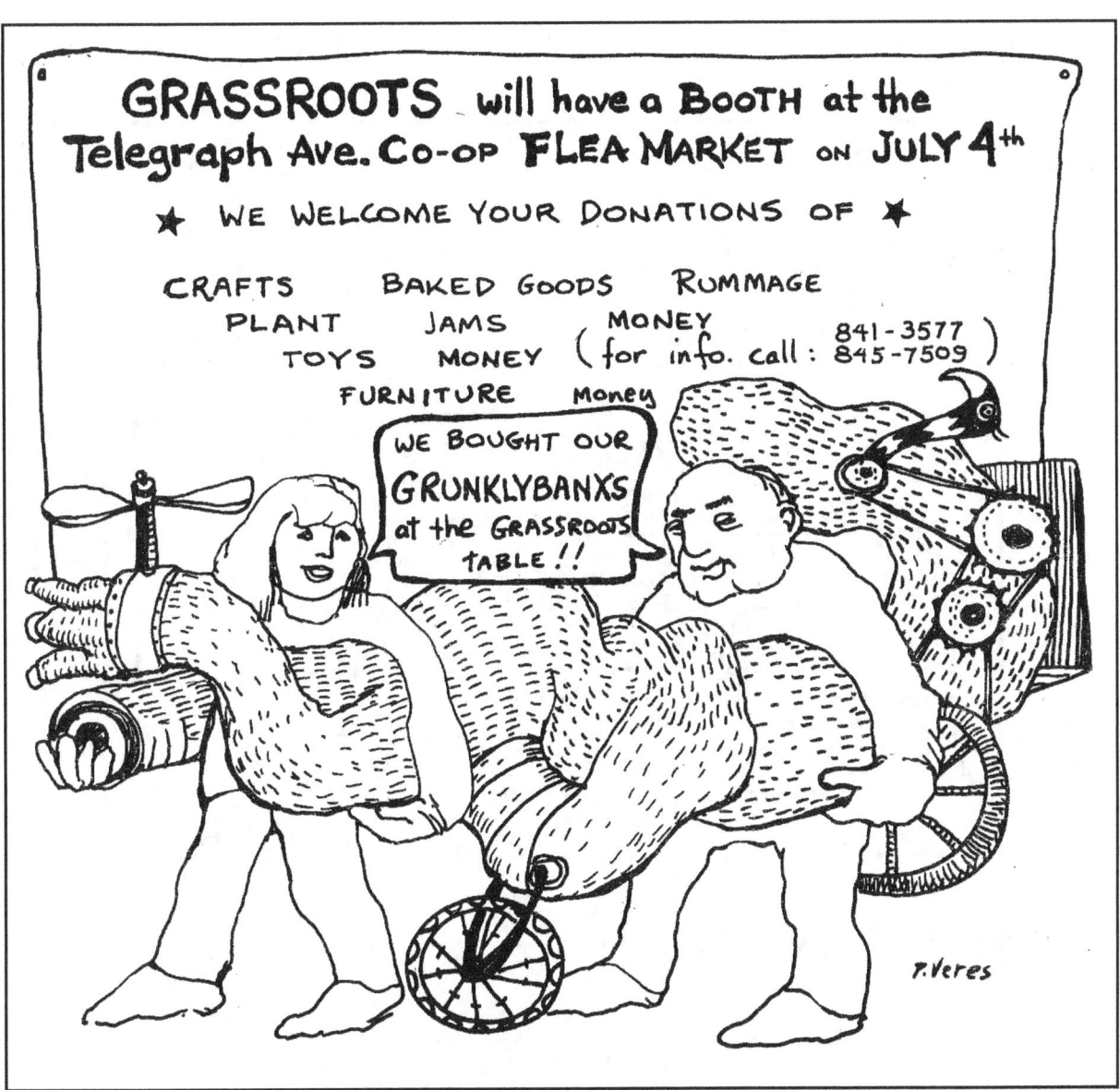

The constant need for money. I don't know how much Grassroots got for the GRUNKLYBANXS.

Vol. III, No. 3   August 7–20, 1974

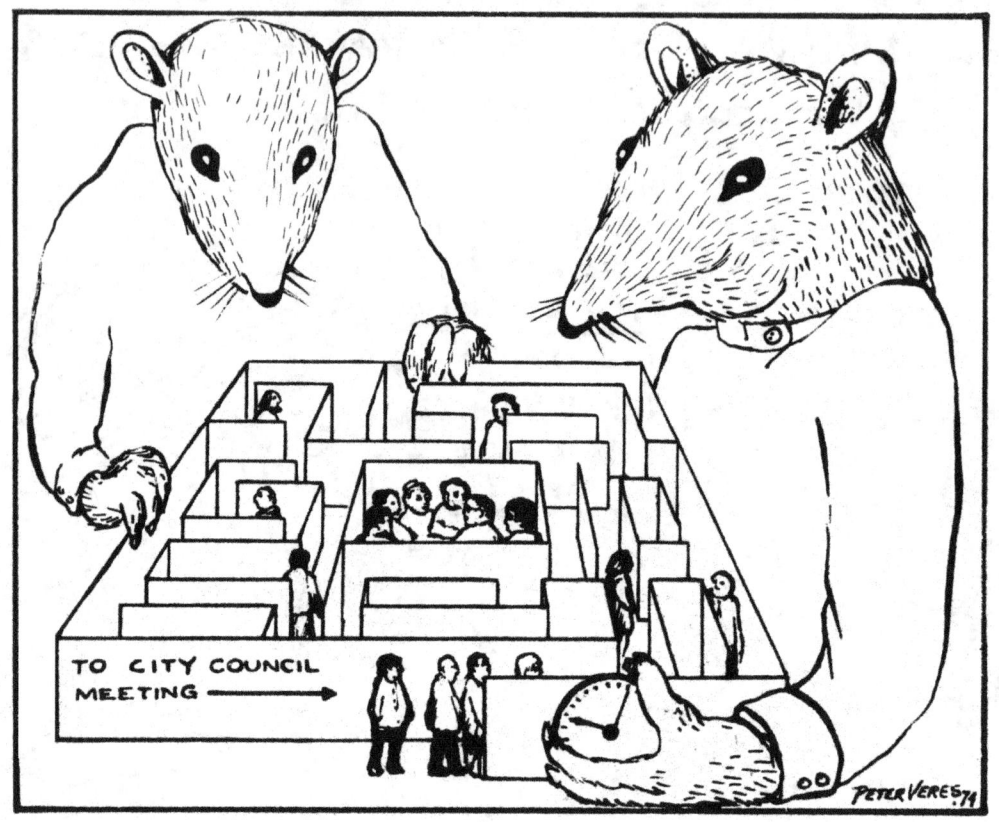

AMAZING MAZE OF CITY COUNCIL PROCEDURE

In the past few weeks the Berkeley City Council has outdone itself in contriving means of meeting to do business and at the same time eluding the public. In fact, the inner logic of the Council has become so fascinating it threatens to take precedence over the business of the Council, that is of "running" the city. The issues now facing the citizens are where and when the Council will meet, and what they will discuss. The great accomplishment is to know this before the meeting.

Time-testing an experiment in democratic representation in Berkeley. To see how long it takes for the citizens to find their representatives.

Vol. 3, No. 7   October 2–15, 1974

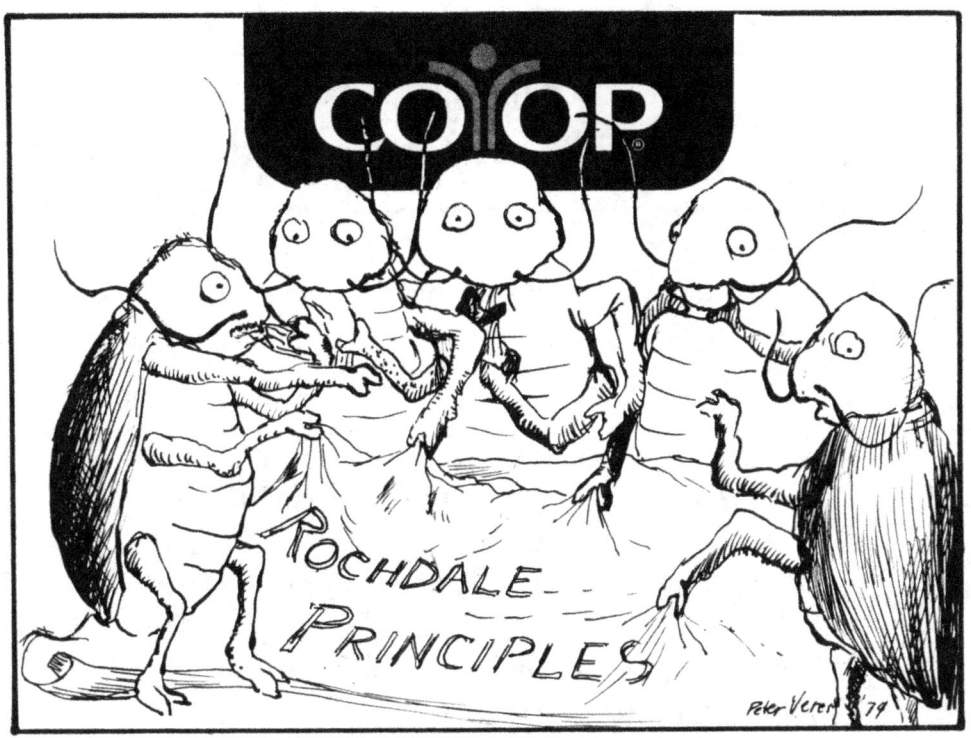

ROACHES IN ROCHDALE?

Apparently, the Co-op's guiding philosophy (a set of principles formulated in the mid-19th century in Rochdale, England, called, consequently, the Rochdale Principles) is subject to local amendment to include denial of due process to and summary dismissal of employees.

In the early morning of September 24, Board Chairman Dave Fleisig announced a surprise executive session (thereby violating the rule requiring prior announcement of such meetings) at which Jerry Rubin moved and Edna Haynes seconded a resolution calling upon Co-op General Manager Roy Bryant to fire Education Director Don Rothenberg. Neither Bryant nor Rothenberg knew that any such move was in the works.

Rubin and Haynes had a number of things to say about their problems with Rothenberg, but most important seems to be an objection to his attempts to increase membership by attracting the "wrong kind of people," i.e., minorities and hippies. A 5-4 majority, including one director who commutes from far away only for matters of special interest to the majority (What's this? A local co-op with absentee directors?!), passed the motion.

So far, Rothenberg has not actually had to leave his job, as Bryant has not yet

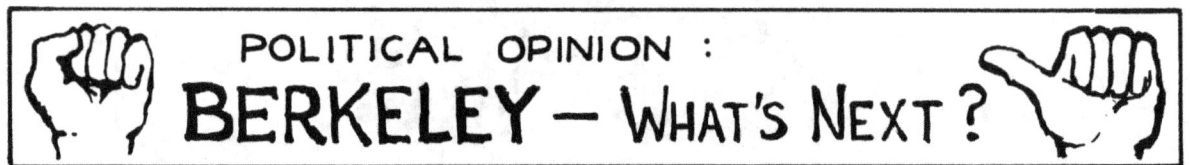

A new column featuring interviews focusing on the issues facing the upcoming April elections.

> Since one of the major problems the Left experienced two years ago was lack of communication within its own ranks, GRASSROOTS has decided that, for the coming months, we will interview people representative of different orientations within the Berkeley Left with the purpose of clarifying our differences and similarities.
>
> We will ask all the people we interview the same series of five questions.

Vol. III, No. 9 November 6-19, 1974

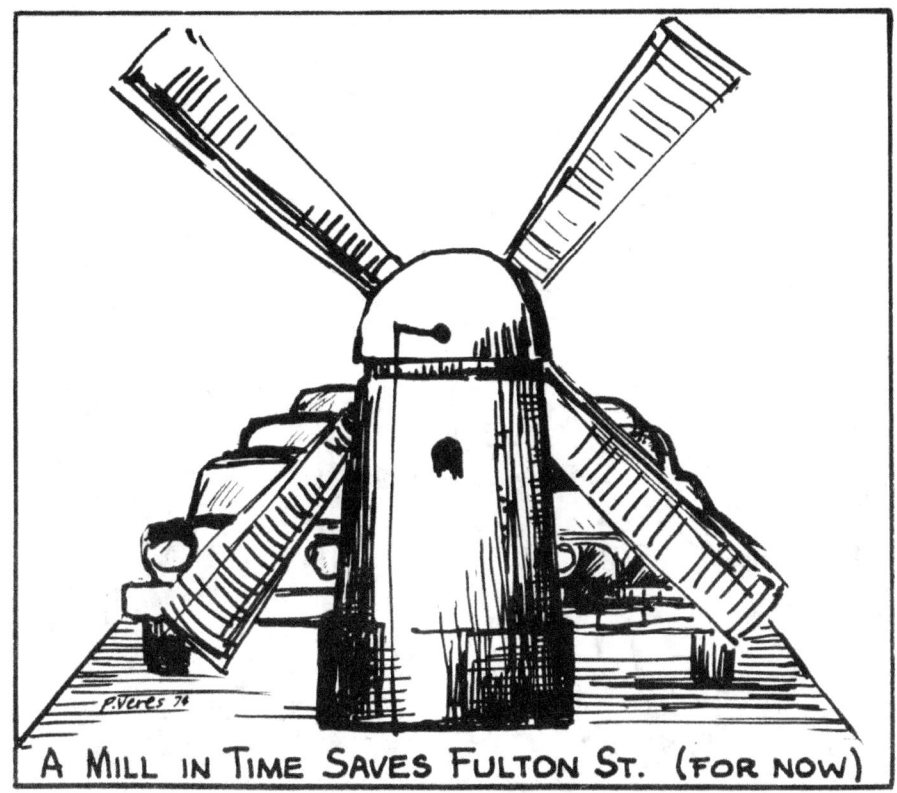

A MILL IN TIME SAVES FULTON ST. (FOR NOW)

CITIZEN ACTION GETS RESULTS

For years the residents in the area surrounding the "Fulton Freeway" have tried to move the city to do something about their problems of too much traffic and too few parks. They have been treated more like prospects for urban renewal than like a lively, important neighborhood. These neighbors have a long history of working through "proper channels" which has gotten them nowhere. A Walker Street Plus park proposal has been dumped from several city budgets because the money just couldn't be found. A city with $140,000 to spend on a traffic study, with $230,000 available for refurbishing a single baseball diamond doesn't have $14,000 to build a small park for children? Parker Street proposals have likewise been scuttled. People spent months in countless meetings with the city's overpriced traffic consultants — at the end of which time the proposal of the engineers from San Francisco did not include the recommendations of the neighbors from Berkeley.

It is easy to see why frustration at such inaction moves people out into the streets. It is not so easy to understand the City's reaction to this frustration. Police response to the first mill-ins was ridiculous and dangerous. As one observer commented: "Chief Pomeroy may have handled 400,000 at Woodstock, but he couldn't deal with 40 on Fulton St." Even at the relatively peaceful Halloween mill-in the police seemed unable to keep one passer-by from charging through the crowd in his car.

However, on October 31 city officials met with area residents and at least the traffic problem may finally be dealt with. We hope that the temporary closure of Fulton and Ellsworth will lead to a permanent solution that meets the neighborhood's needs. It is sad that people have to put their bodies on the line and risk police violence before their demands are treated seriously.

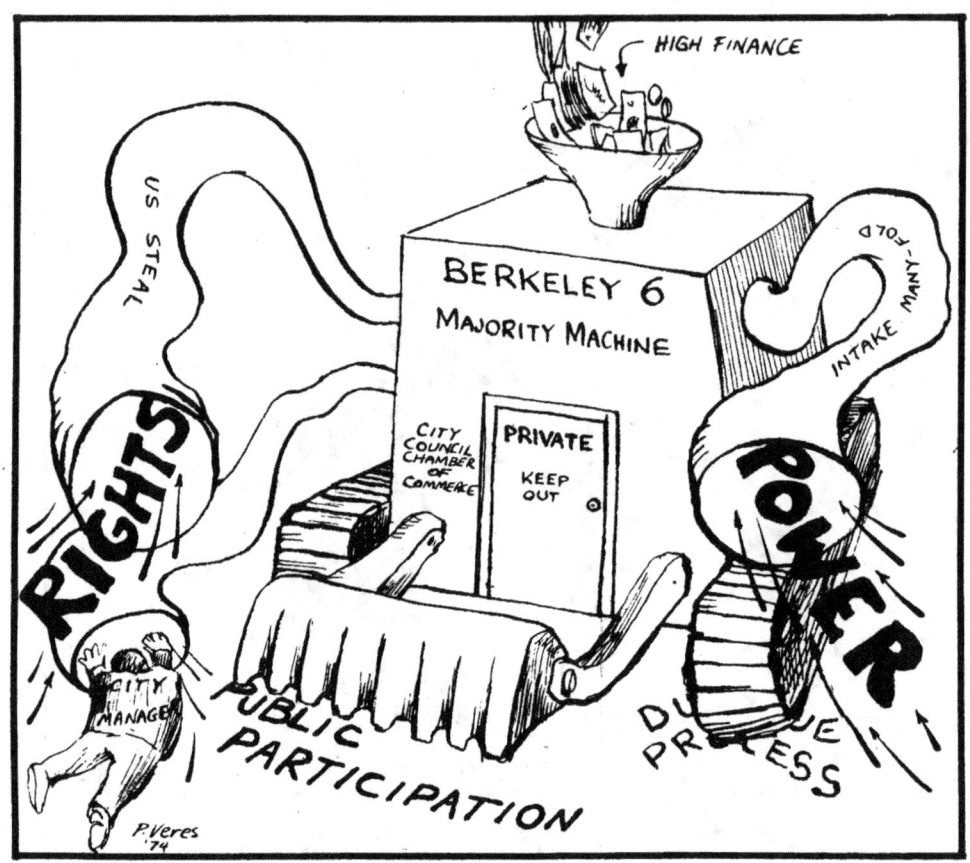

BACKROOM BLUDGEON

That small room behind Berkeley's city council chambers has seen a lot of activity this year. While we are accustomed to seeing our annual budget issue from that den, accompanied by occasional wisps of smoke, other projects, too, have lately come forth from the backroom, to be laid by *fiat* upon a citizenry rendered voiceless by majority arrogance. This time it was city reorganization. Our popular majority has reorganized the bureaucracy — a worthy task indeed — but only as they see fit, with no concern for what best serves the people.

City Manager John Taylor had a reorganization plan, probably not the best in the world, but one that at least benefited from several months of discussion within the city administration and even from a modicum of citizen input. The council majority, however, designed a reorganization plan exclusively on their own. No city departments, none of the three minority council members and no members of the public saw their plan. The only copy came from that cozy backroom, to be read imperiously to the waiting citizen-subjects, then enacted by ramrod vote. In addition to ignoring the public, the Big Six also scuttled Taylor's suggestion for a Citizen Resources Center which would have channeled a public voice into the bureaucracy. There's no room for us folks back there in that privy space.

The council majority "gets it done" alright. "It" is government *on* the people and *at* the people, certainly not for the people.

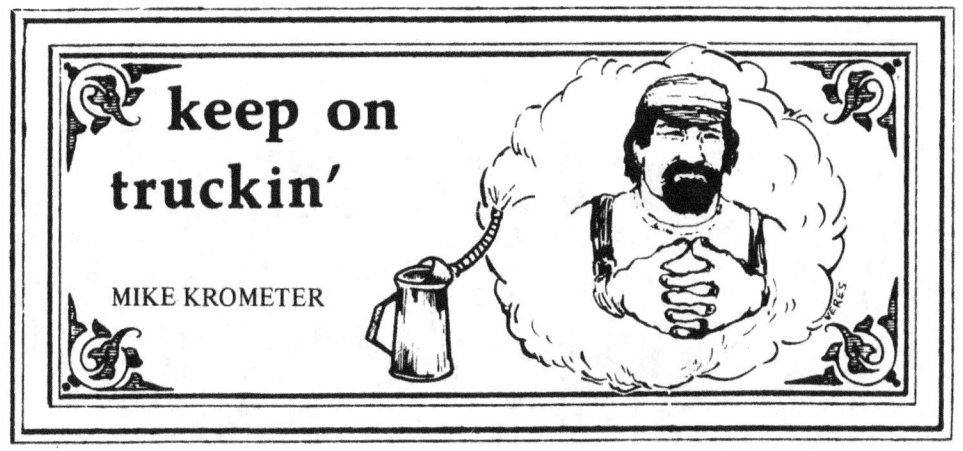

A new logo for **Keep on Truckin'**
The identity of Mike Krometer revealed with Doug Brown's portrait.

Volume III, No. 12   December 18–January 7, 1975

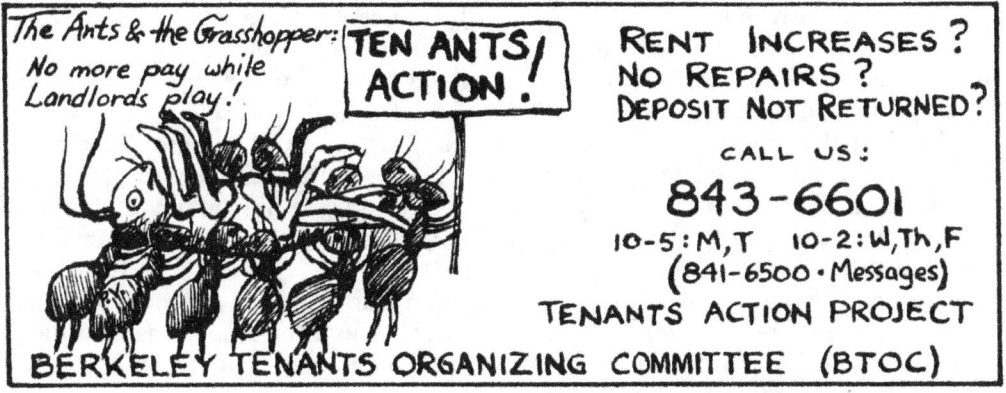

An ad for the Berkeley Tenants Organizing Committee which supported the rights of tenants with legal advice, organized protests, published information on tenants' rights, and worked for the eventual passage of rent control in Berkeley.

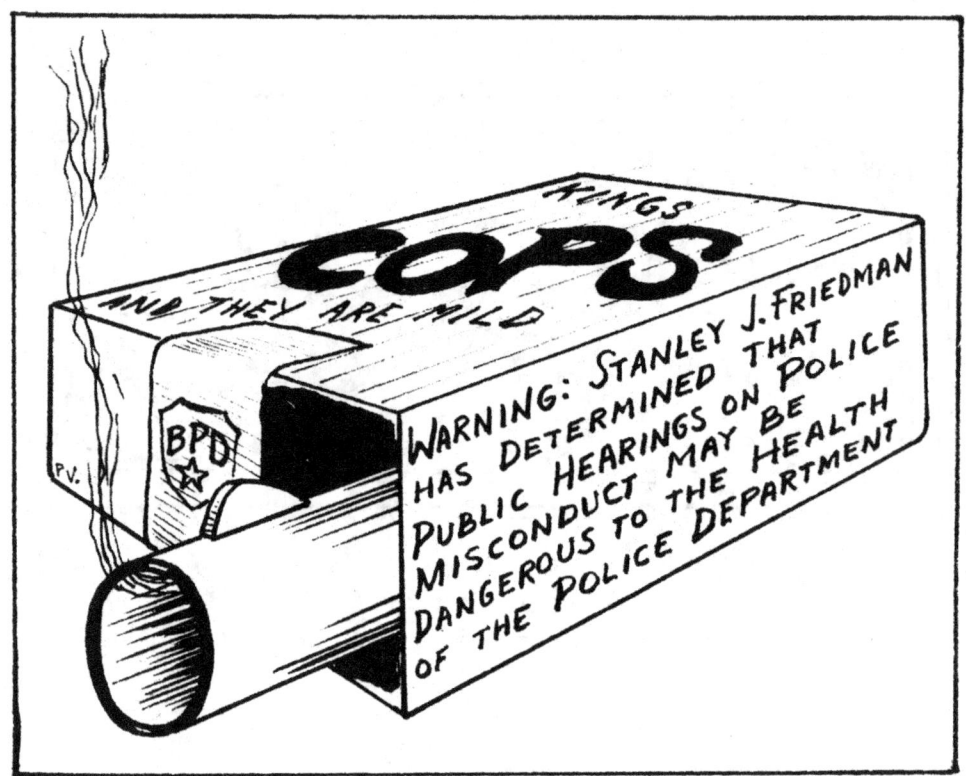

COMMUNITY PROPOSES – FRIEDMAN DISPOSES

One of the most important provisions of the initiative ordinance which established the Police Review Commission requires a public hearing on any incident of alleged police misconduct upon presentation of fifty signatures requesting such a hearing. This provision is fundamental to the concept of community control of police. Now, however, Commissioner Stanley J. Friedman (appointed by Sue Hone) has suggested a new policy on public hearings; a policy which would do much to destroy that concept and perhaps the PRC's public credibility with it.

Friedman has suggested that any public hearings on specific cases of alleged police misconduct be postponed until *after* final resolution of the matter. He has also suggested that if anyone complains about such alleged misconduct at a public hearing, all charges against the accused officers should be dropped; he feels that the airing of such complaints would be prejudicial.

Friedman ignores the fact that any officer complained against can make a public statement at that hearing, too. He also chooses to ignore the reality that the PRC can only recommend action, not order it, so that its primary function is to serve as a sounding board for public sentiment.

Friedman's suggestions could be dismissed as ridiculous if they were not so dangerous. His plan is designed to widen the gap between the people and the PRC, our only legal weapon against police misbehavior. For while the PRC is certainly not all we could wish for in a police control board, it is a start. Furthermore, it is the only electoral victory Berkeley's progressive forces have won in recent years that the conservatives haven't been able to water down or kill outright.

Friedman's suggestions are just one more attempt to destroy the chances of

Vol. III, No. 16   February 20–March 5, 1975

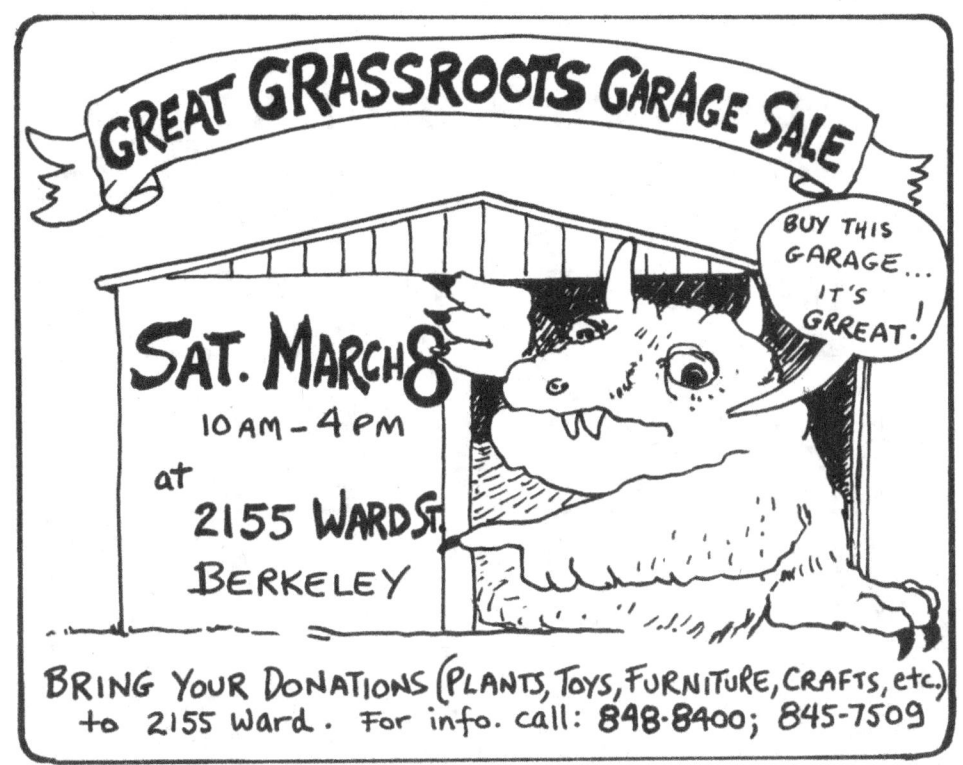

Another money-raising event. Berkeley was a garage sale town.

BALLOT RECOMMENDATIONS

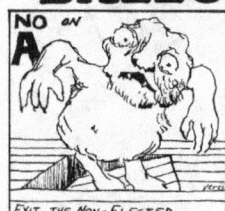

CHARTER AMENDMENT A — Making the ombudsperson independent of the city manager. NO.

In principle we like the idea that he/she be insulated from the bureaucracy, but we would prefer that the position be elective. Also (and more importantly) we expect our council representatives to act as ombudspersons. If the various members of the council are doing their job properly, we would have nine ombudspersons and could save ourselves $31,000 by eliminating this position altogether. Writing the job into the charter would make this more difficult. Therefore, we recommend a NO vote.

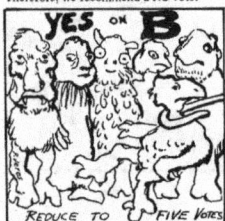

CHARTER AMENDMENT B — Reducing the number of votes needed to fire the city manager. YES.

Grassroots recommends a YES vote on Charter Amendment B to change the number of City Council votes needed to fire the City Manager from 6 to 5. The present requirement of a 6 vote, 2/3 majority of the 9 member council to fire the City Manager makes it nearly impossible to remove any City Manager from office. There is very little opposition to this change which is proposed by the Berkeley Charter Review Committee.

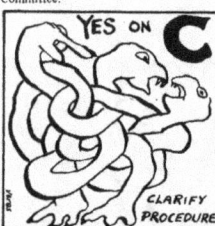

CHARTER AMENDMENT C — Clarifying the Procedure for Issuing Supoenas. YES.

Grassroots recommends a YES vote on Charter Amendment C to revise and clarify the Charter section on oaths and subpoenas. The present section is extremely confusing and it is impossible to tell which city bodies are granted the power to subpoena witnesses and evidence. Charter Amendment C clearly establishes that the subpoena power lies with the City Council and with city boards and commissions when provided by ordinance. Charter Amendment C protects the subpoena power of the Police Review Commission Ordinance and the subpoena power of other boards and commissions. There is no known opposition.

CHARTER AMENDMENT D — Gender changes. YES.

Grassroots recommends a YES vote on Charter Amendment D which makes gender changes in the Charter to eliminate sex-biased terminology. There is no known opposition to this proposal.

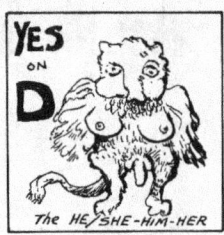

CHARTER AMENDMENT E — City Council confirmation of department heads. YES.

Grassroots recommends a YES vote on Charter Amendment E, the latest in a series of attempts to reduce the power of the City Manager and increase the power of elected officials on the City Council. Under the current Charter the City Manager has total power to appoint all city employees including the powerful positions of city department heads. The City Council has absolutely no say in the appointment of specific people. Under Charter Amendment E, the City Council will have the final say in the appointment of department heads as all department heads proposed by the City Manager will require Council confirmation. Charter Amendment E was proposed by the Berkeley Charter Review Committee. Its opponents include Councilman Ed Kallgren and others who oppose changes in the current City Manager form of government.

GRASSROOTS RECOMMENDS

★★★★ FOR MAYOR ★★★★
- Ying Lee Kelley

★★★★ FOR CITY COUNCIL ★★★★
- Loni Hancock
- John Denton
- Vivian Gales
- Jeff Rudolph
- Mark Allen

★★★★ FOR AUDITOR ★★★★
- Florence McDonald

★★★★ FOR SCHOOL BOARD ★★★★
- Mary Jane Johnson
- Alex Papillon
- Louise Stoll

★★★★ FOR PERALTA COLLEGE BOARD ★★★★
- Rev. A. Edward Bell
- Hynetha Hewitt
- Robert J. Reichert

★★★★ ON BALLOT MEASURES ★★★★
- A-no
- C-yes
- B-yes
- D-yes
- E-yes
- 1-yes
- 2-yes

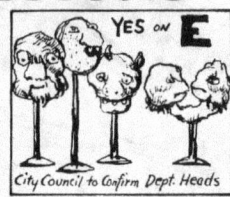

ORDINANCE 1 — Clarification of Police Review Commission terms. YES.

Grassroots recommends a YES vote on Ordinance 1 which is designed to avoid future litigation by amending the Police Review Commission Ordinance to clearly establish the length of Commissioners' terms, the process of appointment, and the method of filling vacancies. In 1973 the City Council majority attempted to make all 9 appointments to the PRC, claiming that the ordinance allowed this. The Alameda County Superior Court held, that the ordinance allowed each Councilmember to make an individual appointment, rejecting the Council majority's claim to monopolize all the appointments. Because the lawsuit delayed the PRC from meeting for several months, there has been a continuing dispute as to the specific date when the Commissioners' two-year terms began. Ordinance 1 solves these problems to the satisfaction of the City Council and the Police Review Commission by specifying the system of individual appointments and the length of terms, thus avoiding another court case. There is no opposition.

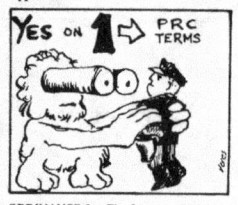
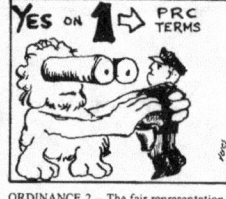

ORDINANCE 2 — The fair representation ordinance. YES, YES, YES.

Grassroots recommends a YES vote on the Fair Representation Ordinance, Ordinance No. 2, to allow all members of the City Council to make appointments to the city's boards and commissions. This is an initiative originated by Councilmembers Ying Kelley and Loni Hancock after the City Council majority began monopolizing all appointments to boards and commissions while totally excluding minority members of the Council from appointing anyone. The problem of arrogant Council majorities monopolizing appointments has gone on for thirty years in Berkeley. The Fair Representation Ordinance corrects this abuse of power by providing for individual appointments by each Councilmember, a practice already followed with the Fair Campaign Practices Commission, the Master Plan Advisory Committee, and the Police Review Commission. This guarantees minority representation, plus fair and equal treatment. The Fair Representation Ordinance is bitterly opposed by the City Council majority.

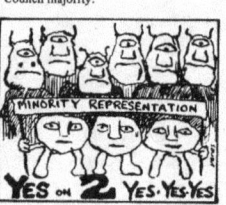

BALLOT RECOMMENDATIONS

Grassroots went through the various ballot measures and gave its recommendations. The verbiage shown below gives some indication of the issues of the day, as well as what I had to work with for illustrations. I enlisted my critters to help me give the proposals a summary and an amusing visual representation.

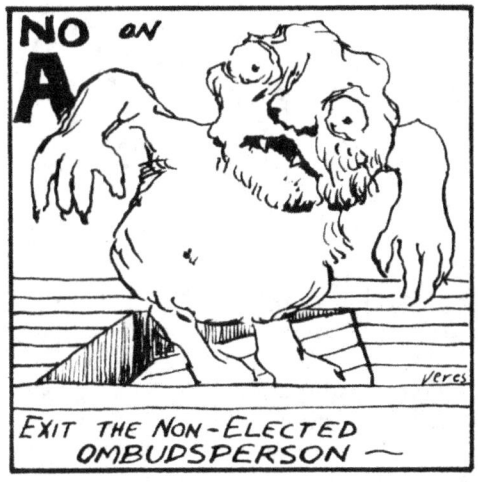

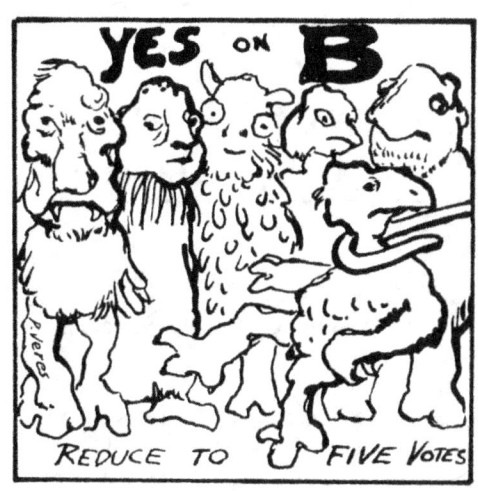

CHARTER AMENDMENT A — Making the ombudsperson independent of the city manager. NO.
In principle we like the idea that he/she be insulated from the bureaucracy, but we would prefer that the position be elective. Also (and more importantly) we expect our council representatives to act as ombudspersons. If the various members of the council are doing their job properly, we would have nine ombudspersons and could save ourselves $31,000 by eliminating this position altogether. Writing the job into the charter would make this more difficult. Therefore, we recommend a NO vote.

CHARTER AMENDMENT B — Reducing the number of votes needed to fire the city manager. YES.
Grassroots recommends a YES vote on Charter Amendment B to change the number of City Council votes needed to fire the City Manager from 6 to 5. The present requirement of a 6 vote, 2/3 majority of the 9 member council to fire the City Manager makes it nearly impossible to remove any City Manager from office. There is very little opposition to this change which is proposed by the Berkeley Charter Review Committee.

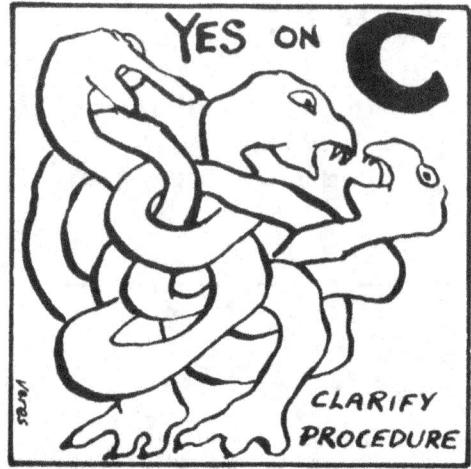 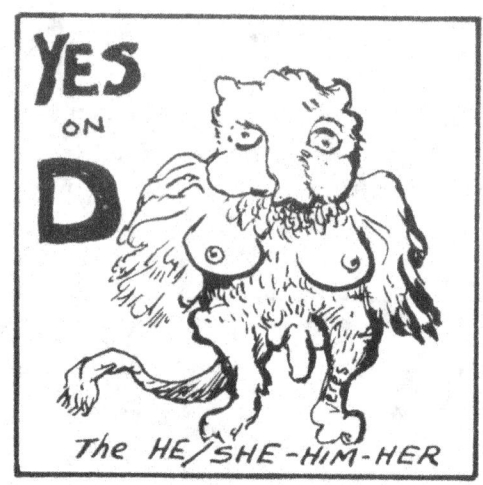

CHARTER AMENDMENT C — Clarifying the Procedure for Issuing Supoenas. YES.

Grassroots recommends a YES vote on Charter Amendment C to revise and clarify the Charter section on oaths and subpoenas. The present section is extremely confusing and it is impossible to tell which city bodies are granted the power to subpoena witnesses and evidence. Charter Amendment C clearly establishes that the subpoena power lies with the City Council and with city boards and commissions when provided by ordinance. Charter Amendment C protects the subpoena power of the Police Review Commission Ordinance and the subpoena power of other boards and commissions. There is no known opposition.

CHARTER AMENDMENT D — Gender changes. YES.

Grassroots recommends a YES vote on Charter Amendment D which makes gender changes in the Charter to eliminate sex-biased terminology. There is no known opposition to this proposal.

My image for Amendment D was another one of those drawings which some people in the collective objected to on the grounds that it might offend some readers. But how better to illustrate the change from male designations to non-sex-biased terms than to show a critter as a He/She-Him-Her Beast?

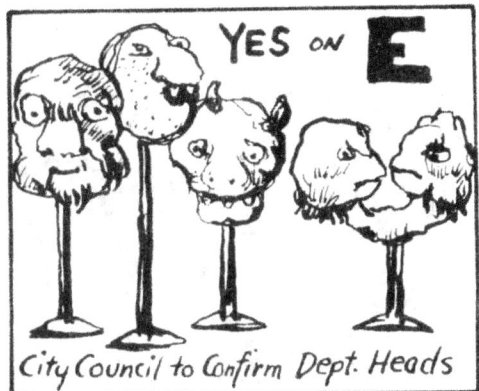

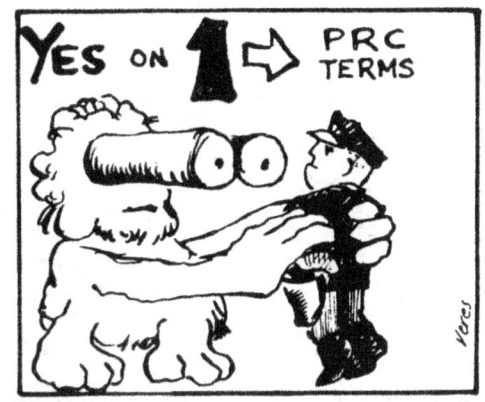

CHARTER AMENDMENT E — City Council confirmation of department heads. YES.

Grassroots recommends a YES vote on Charter Amendment E, the latest in a series of attempts to reduce the power of the City Manager and increase the power of elected officials on the City Council. Under the current Charter the City Manager has total power to appoint all city employees including the powerful positions of city department heads. The City Council has absolutely no say in the appointment of specific people. Under Charter Amendment E, the City Council will have the final say in the appointment of department heads as all department heads proposed by the City Manager will require Council confirmation. Charter Amendment E was proposed by the Berkeley Charter Review Committee. Its opponents include Councilman Ed Kallgren and others who oppose changes in the current City Manager form of government.

ORDINANCE 1 — Clarification of Police Review Commision terms. YES.

Grassroots recommends a YES vote on Ordinance 1 which is designed to avoid future litigation by amending the Police Review Commission Ordinance to clearly establish the length of Commissioners' terms, the process of appointment, and the method of filling vacancies. In 1973 the City Council majority attempted to

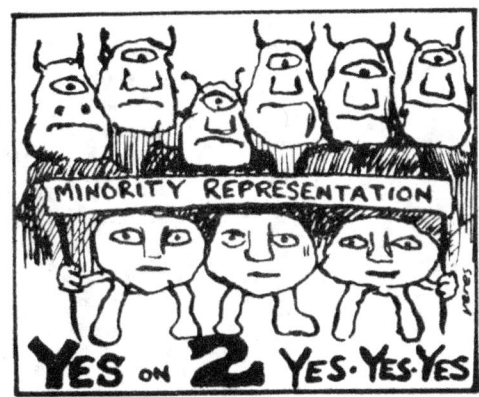

ORDINANCE 2 — The fair representation ordinance. YES, YES, YES.

Grassroots recommends a YES vote on the Fair Representation Ordinance, Ordinance No. 2, to allow all members of the City Council to make appointments to the city's boards and commissions. This is an initiative originated by Councilmembers Ying Kelley and Loni Hancock after the City Council majority began monopolizing all appointments to boards and commissions while totally excluding minority members of the Council from appointing anyone. The problem of arrogant Council majorities monopolizing appointments has gone on for thirty years in Berkeley. The Fair

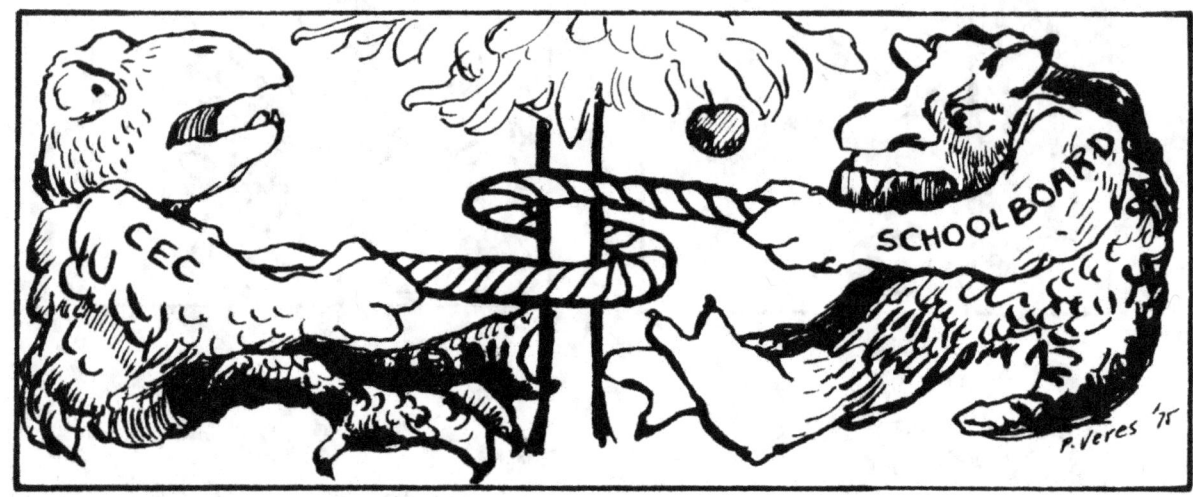

STRIKE THREATENED – TEACHERS PRESENT DEMANDS

In a 532-40 vote at the March 10th meeting called by the Certificated Employees Council (CEC — the body that represents teachers in negotiations with the School Board), teachers decided to strike April 3 if the School Board does not move closer to accepting CEC's recommendations on the following six issues.

1. SALARIES: CEC is asking for a 10 percent increase; the Board would agree to offer 5 percent if state money can be made available. Otherwise they say they can only afford to offer a 3 percent raise. CEC notes that the cost of living has gone up more than 5 percent and calls the Board's offer "a firm offer of nothing."

The other issues covered by this article dealt with the reduction of class sizes, the transfer of teachers, the status and salaries of substitute teachers, and the salaries of early childhood education personnel.   I just showed a tug-of-war around the old apple tree of knowledge.

Vol. III, No. 20   April 23–May 6, 1975

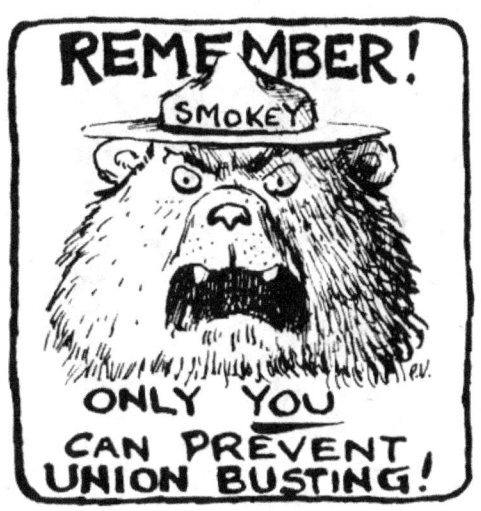

PARK CHIEFS REBUFF STRIKERS

As the weather cleared over the past week-ends and local residents drove to the East Bay Regional Parks for a day of picnics and hiking, they were greeted with some unusual sights. At Tilden they found the Nature Area picketed by the naturalists, at Coyote Hills the gardeners handed them strike bulletins and at the Don Castro Equestrian Center they were asked to sign petitions.

The reason for this is that the naturalists, gardeners, horse handlers and the other 185 members of Local 2428 of the American Federation of State, County and Municipal Employees are striking the East Bay Regional Parks District (EBRPD) in an attempt to protect and preserve their union. The District's management, according to union representatives, has consistently refused to participate in the most basic bargaining activity. The strike is not over economic issues but rather over job representation.

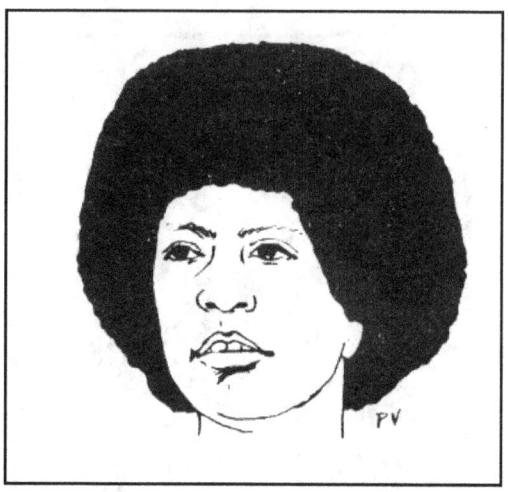

AN INTERVIEW WITH MARGOT DASHIELL

There's still a lot of confusion about what really happened in last month's elections. The winners and losers are pretty obvious, but the subtleties of who gained and who lost strength, and why, are still being debated. To get one side of the story, we talked to Margot Dashiell, who waged an unsuccessful council campaign in 1973 under the banner of the old April Coalition. Margot has not finished studying precinct results yet, but she had some very definite ideas about the way Berkeley Citizens Action (BCA) was set up and how it ran the campaign.

BLACK PARTICIPATION IN BCA

"I think a Black left organization (within BCA) would have made a difference," she said, "but you can't expect Black participation unless there is Black leadership." She noted that "a number of unfortunate things" happened to prevent that from coming about.

"There's a sense among the people who formed BCA that it's best to select candidates out of a coalition in which whites predominate, rather than to allow Black groups to select their candidates separately, which was the idea of the 1971 Coalition. The people who now make up BCA scrapped that idea unilaterally."

Margot noted that the April Coalition reversed its position in 1973, and that the Black Caucus (whom she represented

Vol. III No. 22   May 21–June 2, 1975

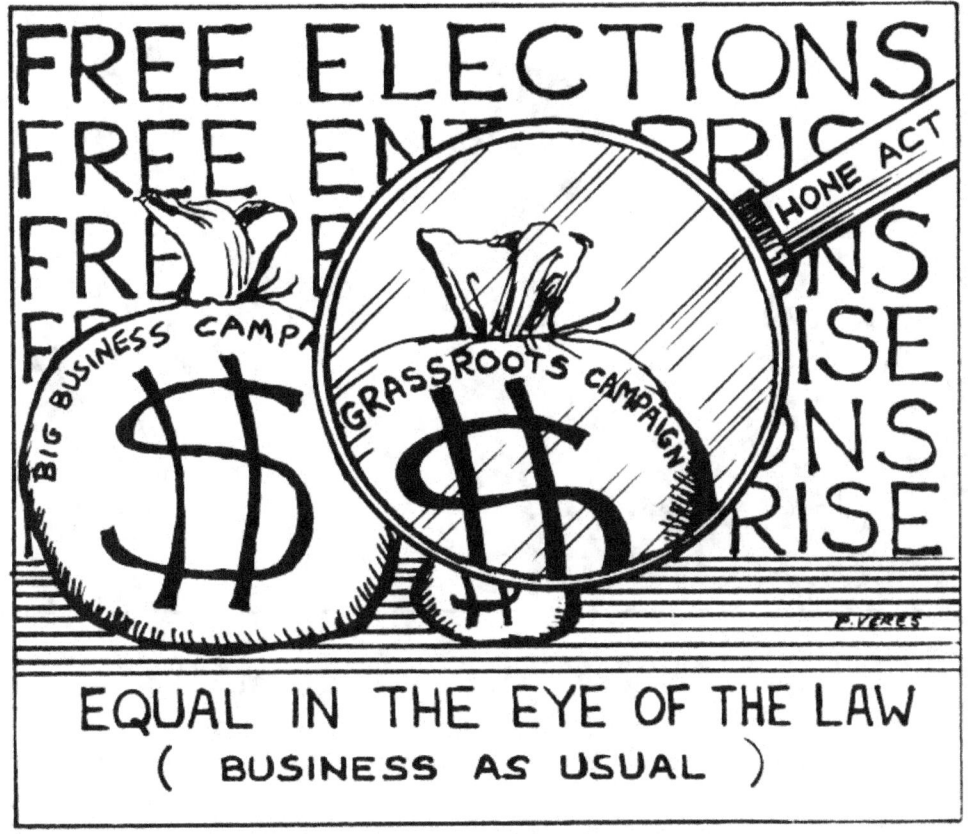

CAMPAIGN FINANCIAL ANALYSIS
DEMOCRATIC CLUB OUTSPENDS BCA 2 TO 1

The final report on campaign fund raising and spending is not due until mid-June. Even so it seems certain that spending by the Berkeley Democratic Club slate was down substantially from the approximately $80,000 spent by their political forbears, "The Berkeley Four," two years ago.

Spending by the BCA candidates was about the same as the April Coalition slate of '73 ($17,000). What this adds and subtracts to is that this time around we were outspent 2 or 3 to 1 instead of the 6 or 8 to 1 of past elections.

The profile of the BCA fund-raising

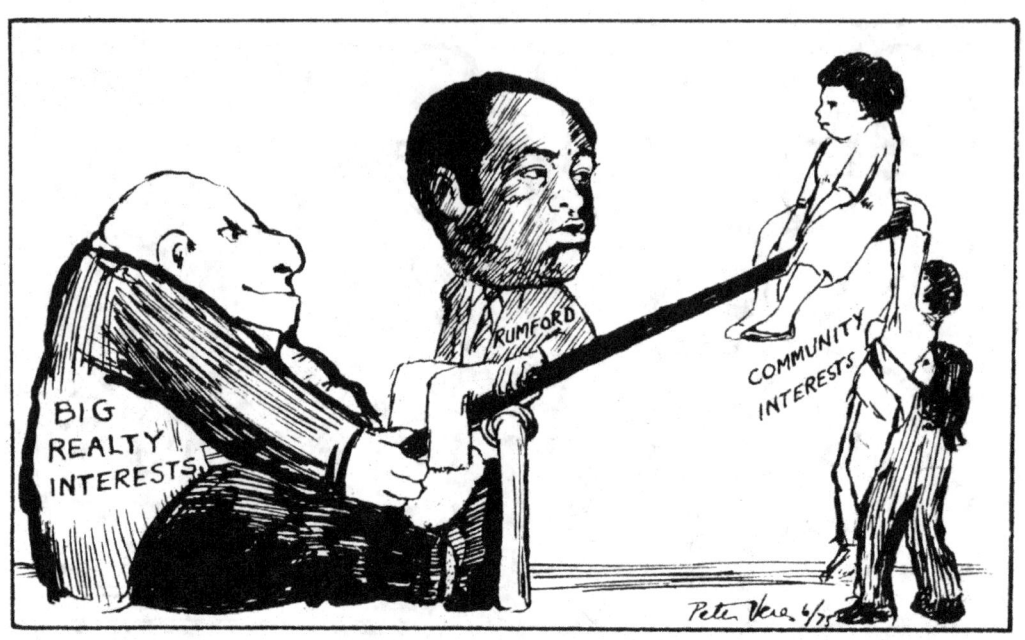

WHAT A DIFFERENCE A WEEK MAKES

For a moment, it seemed as though a wave of change was ready to sweep Berkeley. Two meetings ago, the City Council voted to take control of the Berkeley Redevelopment Agency and to decide the future of the West Berkeley Industrial Park project.

But no. On second reading this week the council rescinded its original motion and were willing to leave the project in the hands of the same inept group which has drained the city of millions. Shirley Dean's statements and questions during the discussion indicated a real concern for the destruction of the Oceanview community and the failures of the BRA, which has never been audited.

When the issue finally came to a vote, Councilmembers Carole Davis, Sue Hone, Henry Ramsey and Mayor Warren Widener voted to support continued real estate control of the BRA. Councilmembers Shirley Dean, John Denton, Loni Hancock and Ying Lee Kelley voted against and supported the original proposal for council control.

Councilmember Rumford, who had originally voted with the majority, turned around the following week to reverse his decision. If Rumford thought the idea was a good one on first reading, then what or who changed his mind??

Many here feel that his change of vote is an indication that real estate and big business interests still call the shots. Fourteen houses scheduled for demolition in Oceanview are again threatened. But this comes as no surprise. It's just that many of us wanted to believe that there was, in fact, hope for the people of Berkeley who have gone unrepresented in matters which vitally concern them.

Willam B. Rumford Jr. was the son of William Byron Rumford, the first African American elected to any public office in Northern California, and the author of the Rumford Fair Housing Act which, when passed in 1963, ended housing discrimination in California.

Vol. III, No. 24   June 18–July 1, 1975

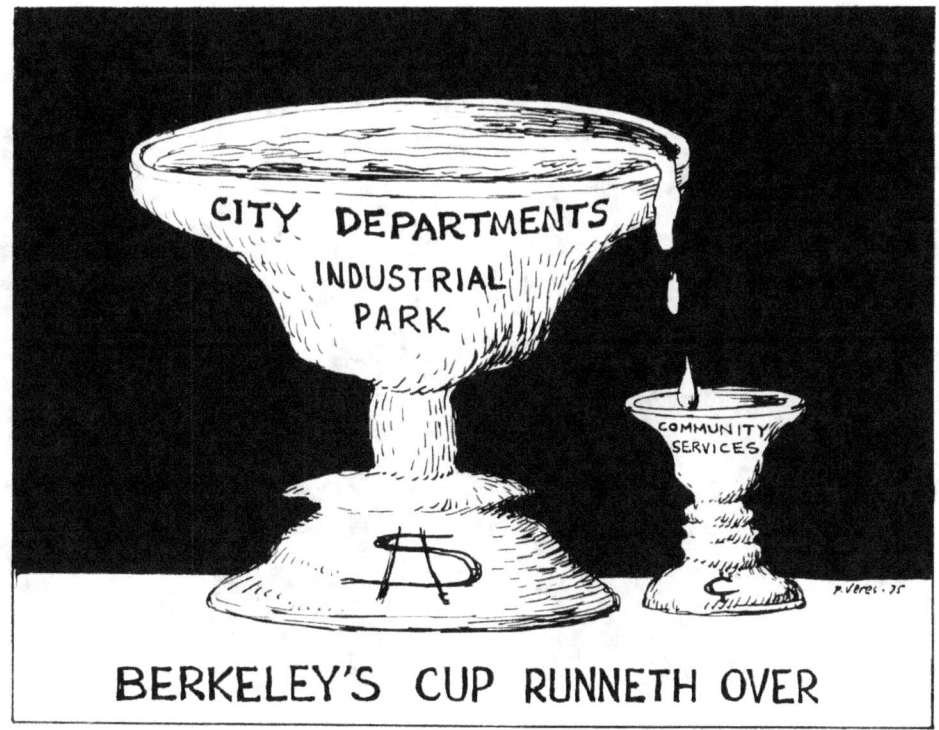

CRUMBS FOR SOCIAL SERVICES ?

The City of Berkeley spends a lot of money — this year, around $48 million. Yet the money never goes to the right places. Community agencies which provide low cost, community-oriented social services continue to get the short end of the stick. Under the leadership of Community Services United and Project Upgrade, many of these agencies have worked together to improve service delivery to many sectors of the community — a task the city itself has not done. This year for the first time a significant number of agencies in South and West Berkeley are applying for city funding.

But the City Manager and the Council majority have other priorities. Once again, they will fail to provide the people of Berkeley with the services they so desperately need. Community agencies, required to go through a lengthy evaluation process, are told they will have to settle for a total of $500,000, which is about one third of what they actually need. City departments have never been evaluated, but continue to get increased funding every year. The City Council pours money into the West Berkeley Industrial Park, and then claims it can't find the money for needed social services. It refuses to push for tax reform and the municipalization of PG&E, and announces there are no funds available.

And Berkeley is not unique. Cities across the country are in the midst of a financial crisis, and social services, particularly needed at this time, are the first cut. On the national level, defense appropriations continue to rise, while the ranks of the unemployed increase.

I had already shown John Taylor brushing crumbs from a bowl (page 54), so here I used wine, showing the trickle-down factor before that phrase became Reaganomics' rationale in the 1980s.

Vol. IV, No. 1   July 2-15, 1975

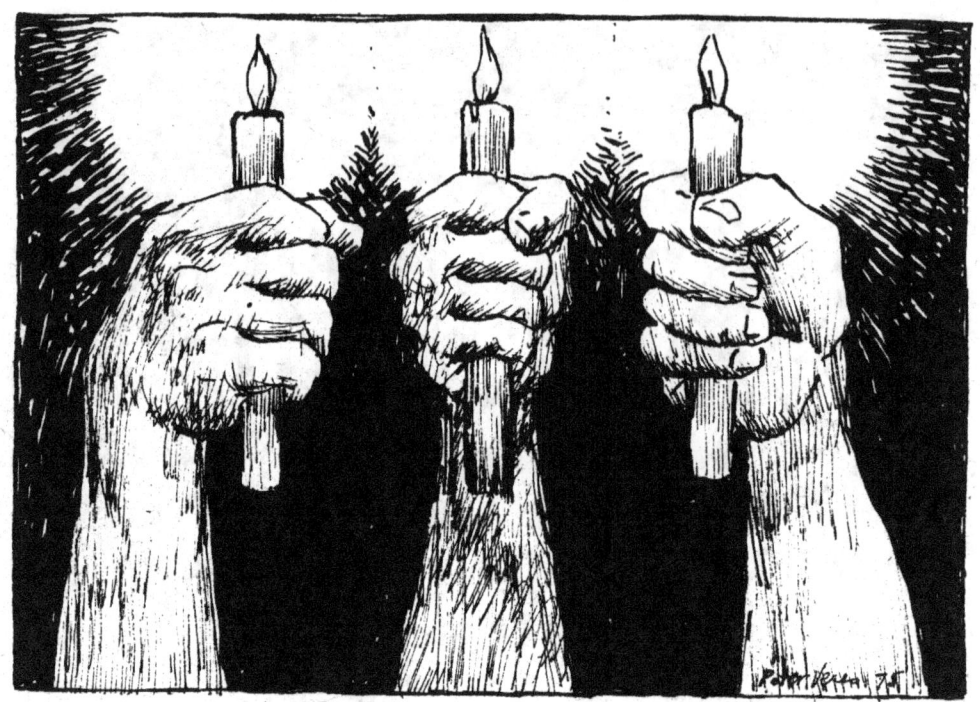

WE'RE 3 YEARS OLD WHERE'S OUR PRESENT?

With this issue, GRASSROOTS celebrates its third birthday. Three years is a long time for a volunteer, collective effort to survive and we are proud of what we are doing.

This year we plan more coverage on Third World community activities in Berkeley. We need more contact with grassroots organizations that we have not covered well, and we need to strengthen contacts with our old friends.

But it takes a lot of time and money to put out even a single issue of GRASSROOTS. Because we manage to come out every two weeks and look sharp, people begin to relate to us as they would to any other newspaper, but we really are quite different. A quick glance at our books would tell you that we do not rely on advertisers or big bankrollers to keep this show going. Our only reliable financial base is our subscribers and occasional small donors. Money is a constant struggle and we can ALWAYS use more.

GRASSROOTS is different from other newspapers. It is no accident that many of the articles in GRASSROOTS are contributed by people's organizations. GRASSROOTS is the place where those groups working for radical political change speak to the community in their own voices.

GRASSROOTS is different because we openly take sides on the issues we cover. We stand with the tenants, farmworkers, rent strikers, health collectives, striking workers, and neighborhood groups against big business, real estate interests, and their representatives in the media and city hall.

We know that our survival isn't something we've done all by ourselves. Without the financial and moral support of the progressive community in Berkeley, we would have folded long ago. So HAPPY BIRTHDAY to you too.

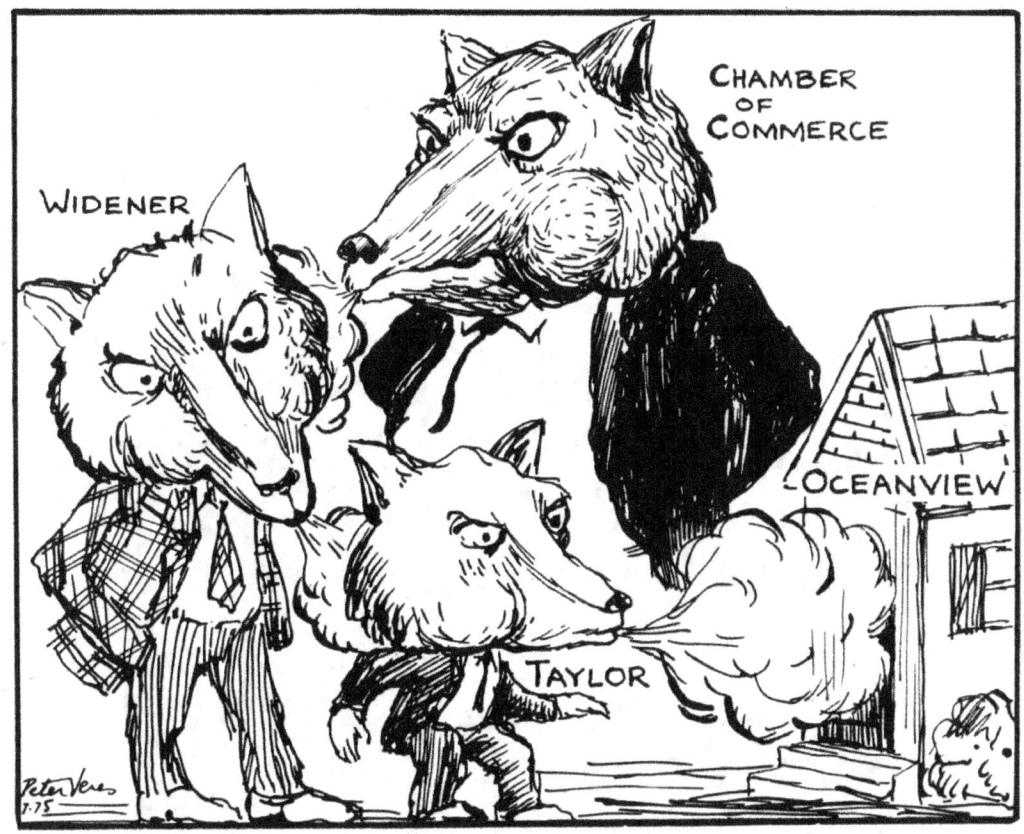

WHAT MAKES TAYLOR RUN?

City Manager John Taylor said he wouldn't order the demolition of eight houses in Oceanview because they were found to be in "repairable condition" and therefore protected by the Neighborhood Preservation Ordinance.

But Mayor Widener put the screws on and Taylor changed his mind. Widener refused to sign a bank note needed to keep the city running unless Taylor ordered the demolitions. Taylor explained his change of heart by saying that the homes are a health and safety hazard.

The Mayor's interest in the Berkeley Redevelopment Agency pork barrel in Oceanview is just another example of his commitment to the Chamber of Commerce. They're the only people in town who think the Industrial Park is a good thing. So the Chamber pulls Widener's strings and Widener pulls John Taylor's.

Don't let these homes be destroyed. Councilpeople Denton, Kelley, and Hancock have asked the court to halt the demolitions. The Mayor, Rumford, Ramsey, Hone and Davis are intent on destroying the homes. Let your Council and Mayor know how you feel. The Mayor has a phone: 644-6484.

Vol. IV, No. 3   August 6-19, 19

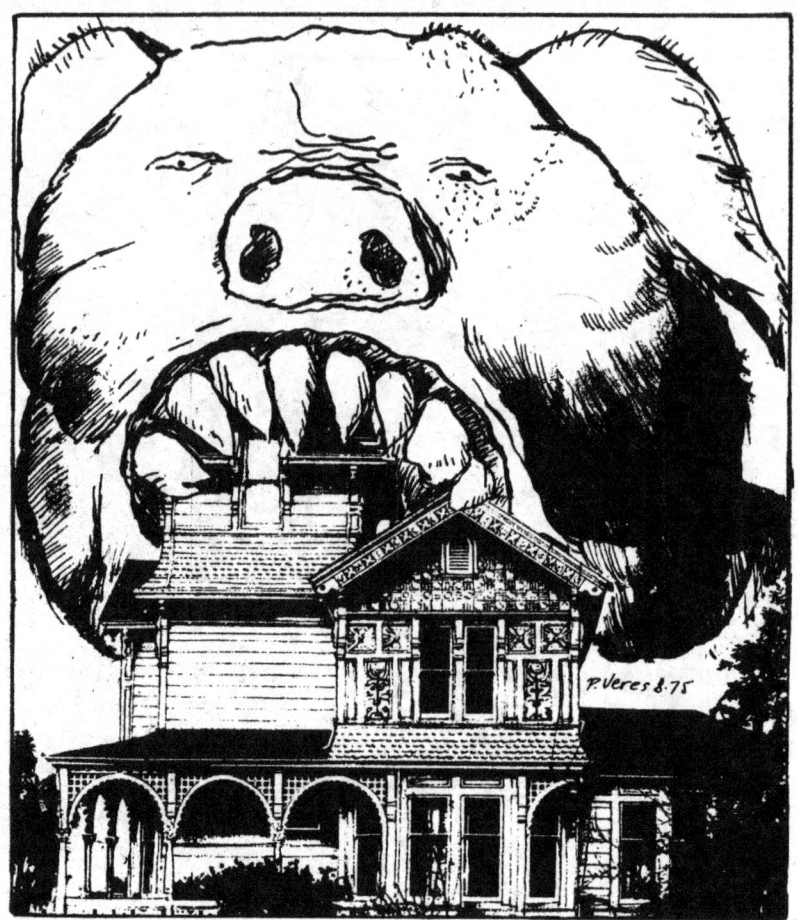

CALL THE B.R.A. TO ACCOUNT

The arrests of ten people who tried stopping the "temporary" moving of a house in Oceanview has dramatized Berkeley's housing plight. The moving and boarding up of this once habitable house by the Berkeley Redevelopment Agency (BRA) is an example of the waste created in the name of bringing new business to Berkeley. The house moved Friday stood on the same block as a company which recently moved to South San Francisco. Is this bringing business to Berkeley? Is this easing the housing shortage?

The BRA's own commissioned audit alleges criminal liability in the agency's books. This comes as no surprise to readers of *Grassroots*, who are aware of conflicts of interest and questionable payment practices by the BRA.

The BRA must be stopped, and it must be thoroughly investigated. In a final City Council vote to take control of the BRA in May, William Rumford changed his vote, halting the action. Rumford argued then that he was awaiting the audit. With the audit now public, we urge Councilman Rumford to reconsider his vote.

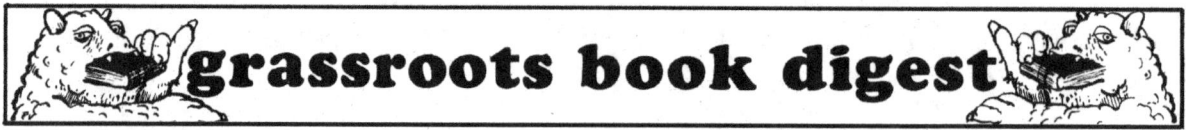

A logo for a book review column.

Vol. IV, No. 8   October 22–November 4, 1975

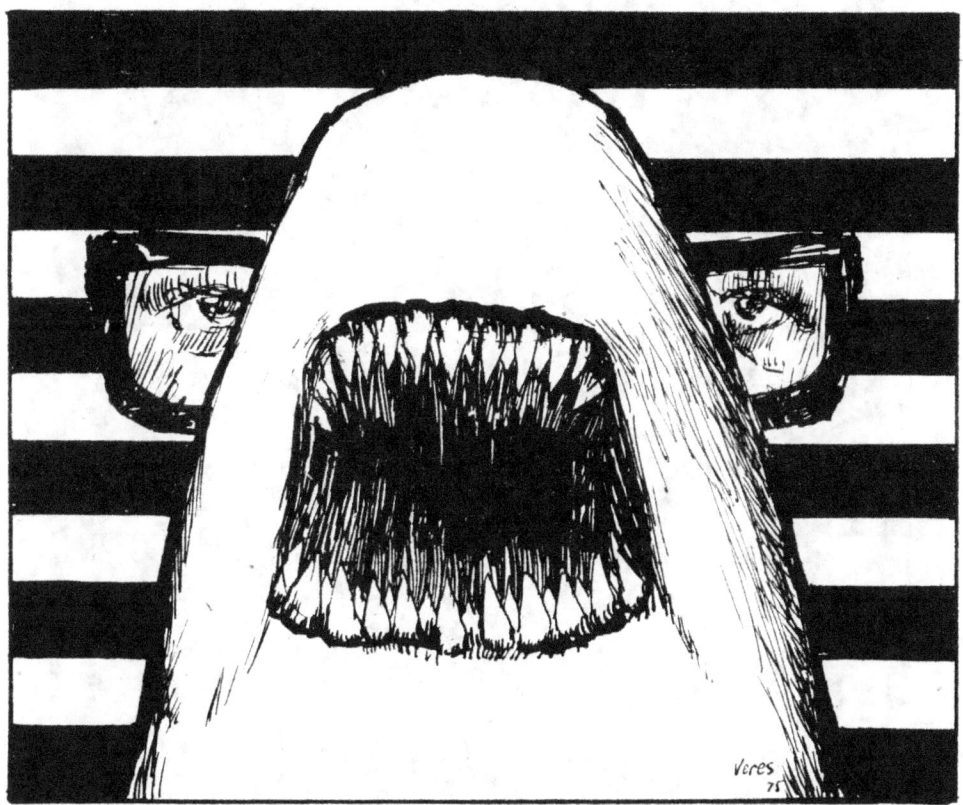

PRESENTING HENRY K., FOR NELSON & CO.

There was no story in this issue of Grassroots about Henry Kissinger or Nelson Rockefeller, but there must have been something in the news about the lethal Henry, who was promoted through his deep connections to Rockefeller to become Nixon's National Security Advisor and Secretary of State, and was a major force in the United States' war against Vietnam. He was also instrumental in that earlier September 11 terrorist attack, in 1973, the military coup that destroyed Allende's government in Chile. So this was my own editorial for Grassroots.

Vol. IV, No.10   November 19–December 9, 1975

> THE SCHOOL BOARD
>
> I will not bully, deceive and cover up
> I will not bully, deceive and cover up
> I will not bully, deceive and cover up
> I will not bully, deceive and cover up
> I will not bully, deceive and cover up
> I will not bully, deceive and cover up
> I will not bully, deceive and cover up
> I will not bully, deceive and cover up

CLEAR UP SCHOOL DAZE

To promote community discussion of public education in Berkeley, GRASSROOTS will run a series of documented analyses to reveal what's really happening in the schools and what political forces are shaping district priorities. We are running this series because information about how the district functions is hard to come by, and the school administration deliberately obfuscates the issues.

Among the issues we intend to analyze are:
A) Decentralization and how it can work in Berkeley.
B) Teaching in the Berkeley schools: What's possible now and what should be possible?
C) School of Finance: What's behind the fiscal crisis and how can we get out of it?
D) A position by position analysis of which administrators are necessary for the functioning of a decentralized system.
E) The politics of school employees organizations.
F) Parent-teacher communication.
G) Third World perspective on the Berkeley Unified School District.
H) Aftermath of the strike.

Vol. IV, No. 11   December 10-23, 1975

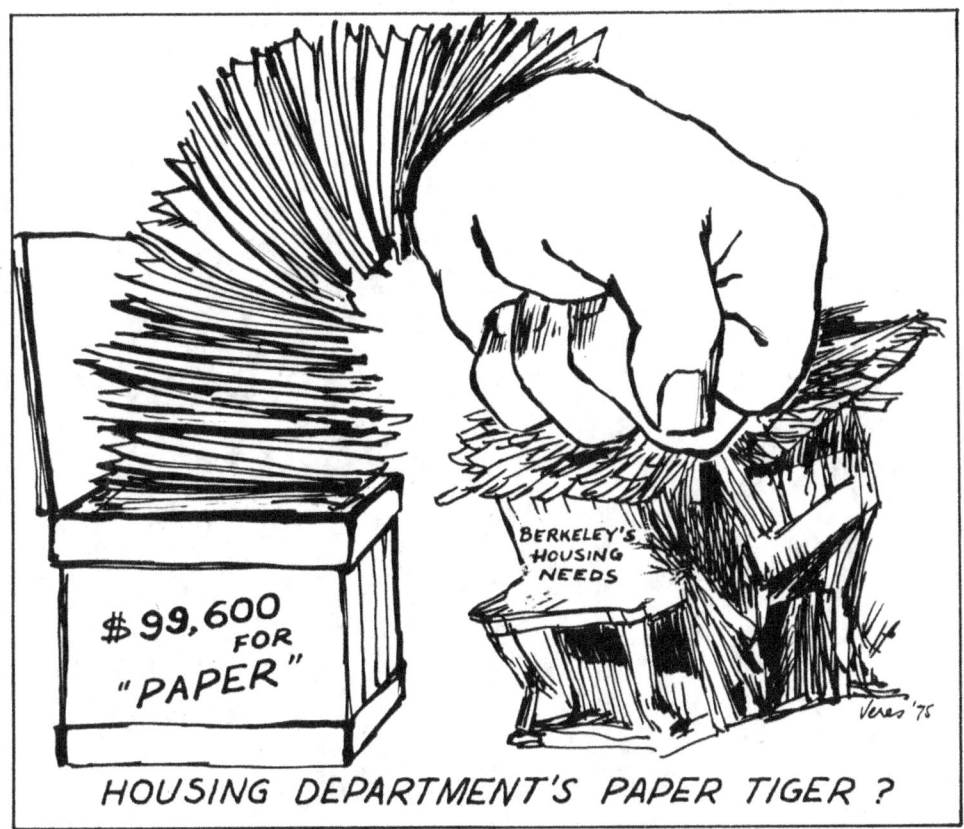

25 MILLION SHEETS ?!!

Berkeley needs a new budget process. A proposal for a Citizens Budget Advisory Committee to work with city staff to analyze the budget failed to pass the City Council. Berkeley needs a proposed budget long before the beginning of the fiscal year, so it can be reviewed by citizens and community groups. Until then, the budget process will be poorly managed, and at worst, secretive and undemocratic.

To take an example, the Housing and Development Department budget passed in October included a simple item: paper, with an allocation of $99,600. At about two dollars a ream, which the city probably pays, this amounts to 49,800 reams, or close to 25 million sheets of paper. For 72 employees in one department, it would be quite a chore to use all this paper in one year. Furthermore, last year's budget for paper totalled $4,550. That indicates a 2,089% increase in the space of one year.

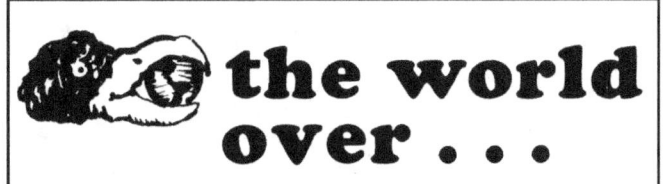

A logo for reports on international stories.

Vol. IV, No. 14 January 28–February 10, 1976

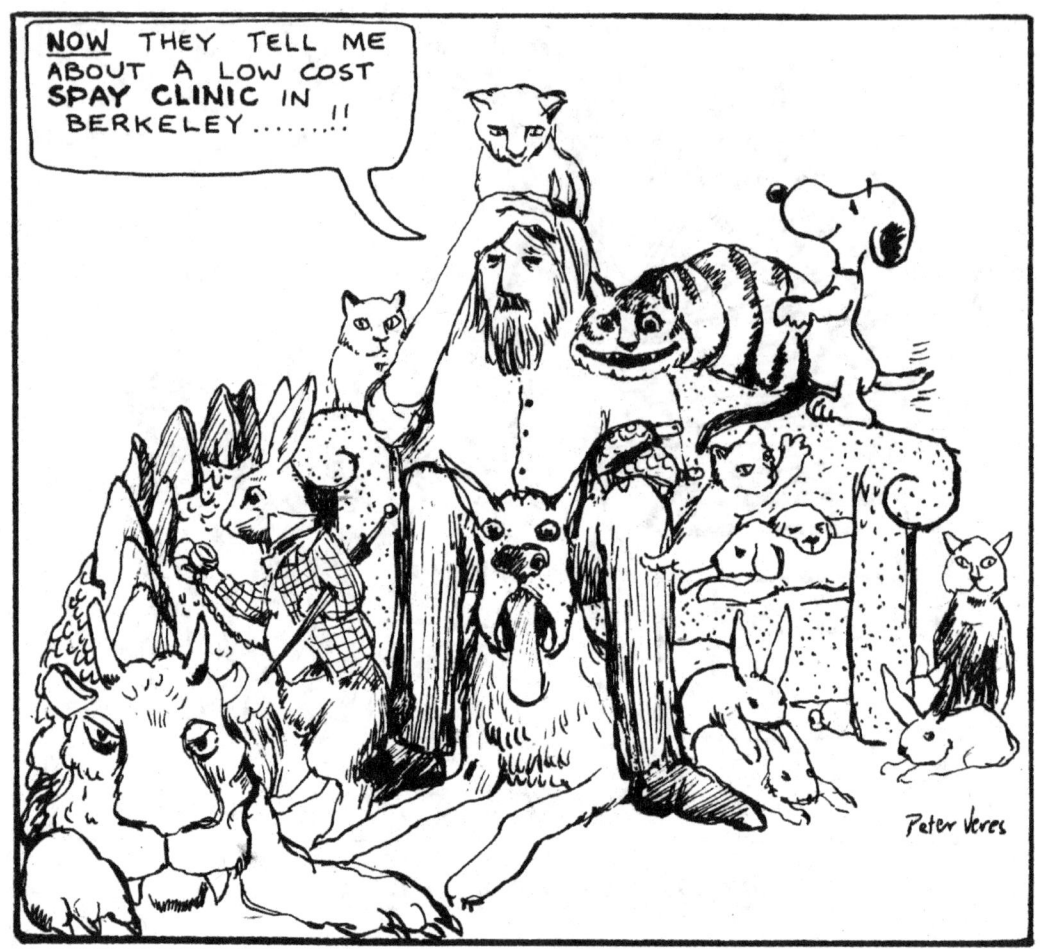

Vol. IV, No. 15 February 11–24, 1976

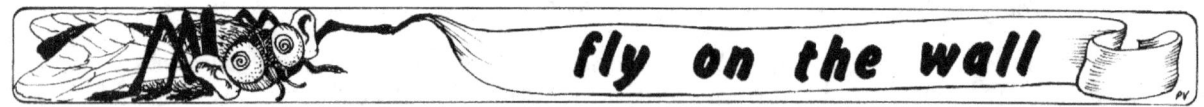

Another design for the Fly on the Wall logo. I don't know why a new one was needed.

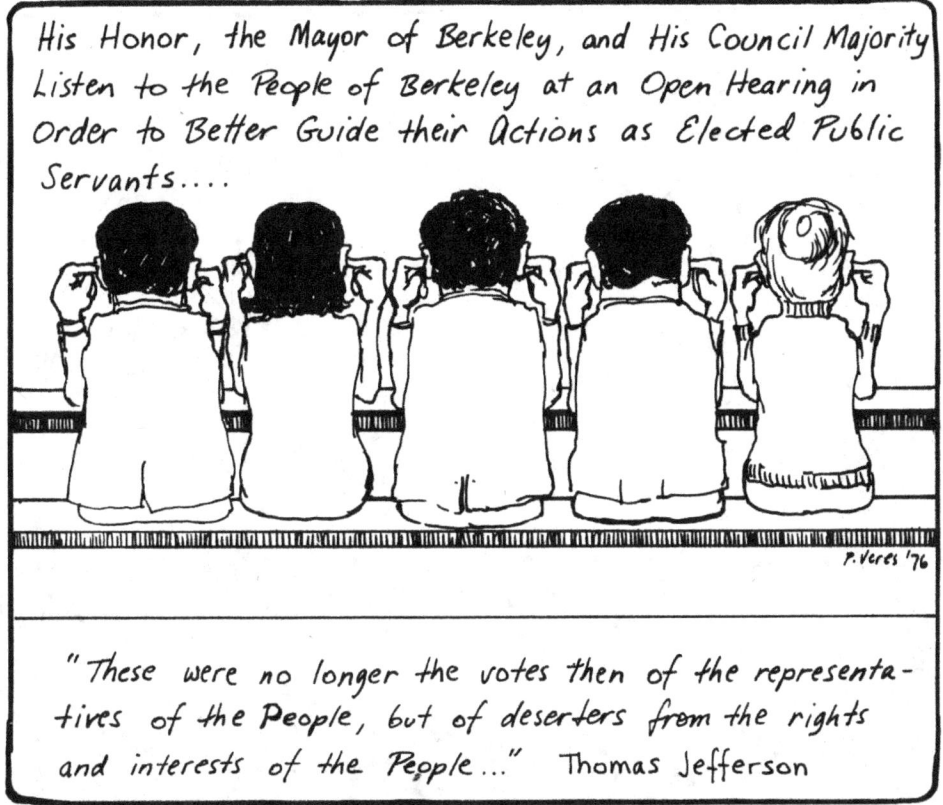

COUNCIL IGNORES NOBBS – EVICTION BY INSPECTION?

Despite the fears and against the wishes of the people who live there, the City Council has imposed the Housing Department's Action Plan for Residential Rental Inspection Program (RRIP) on the North Berkeley BART Station (NOBBS) neighborhood.

HENCE THE TERM 'GLIBERAL'

The council's public hearing on the matter February 17 lasted five hours, but it could have been settled in five minutes. Or maybe even three weeks earlier. When the action plan was first brought before the council, the outcry against it was so strong that Sue Hone and Shirley Dean joined the progressive minority in voting for the public hearing. When the hearing came, however, it became obvious that Hone's vote had been merely for appearance's sake, so that she could seem to be "genuinely concerned" with what people wanted for their own neighborhood, while, ignoring them. Along with Davis, Ramsey, Rumford and

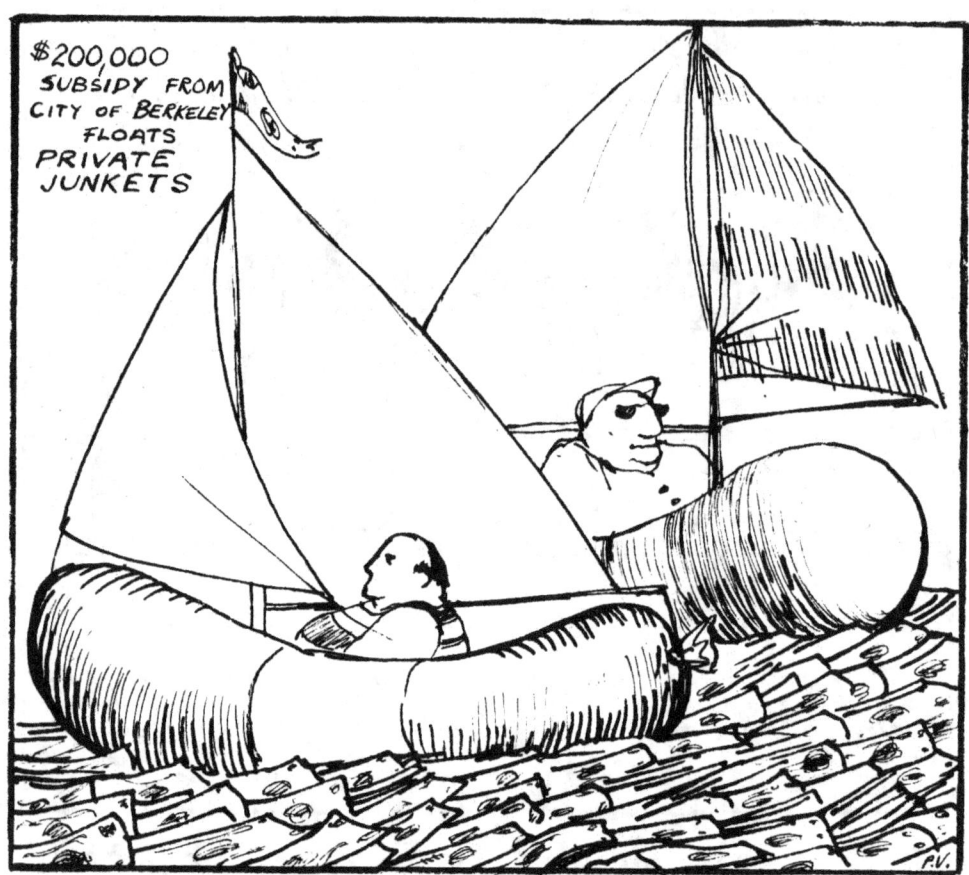

DING THE DINGHY BERTHERS

Let us remind you of a few facts concerning the Berkeley Marina:

Of the more than 1000 boat owners who berth their yachts there, less than one third live in Berkeley. The others come from as far away as Palo Alto, Sacramento and Virginia City, Nevada;

The Berkeley Marina has been judged to be amongst the finest in the Bay Area, with superb facilities, beautiful vistas, and immediate access to the best sailing areas in the Bay;

The berthing rates are the lowest in the Bay Area. At $1.25 per linear foot, it costs less to park your yacht than to buy salami. The rates are so low because the taxpayers of Berkeley cough up about $200,000 annually to subsidize them;

While there are a number of exclusive high-priced watering places in the Marina, there are no low-cost family style restaurants.

All in all, it is a rather familiar story. But we do have a chance to change this scenario. Thanks to the Fair Representation Ordinance, for the first time the Waterfront Advisory Board has some members who are themselves not members of the boating set. We have some really hard-working, dedicated, informed, and community-oriented people who are trying to change the Marina to see that the subsidy of private recreational facilities ceases.

Vol. IV, No. 23   June 2-22, 1976

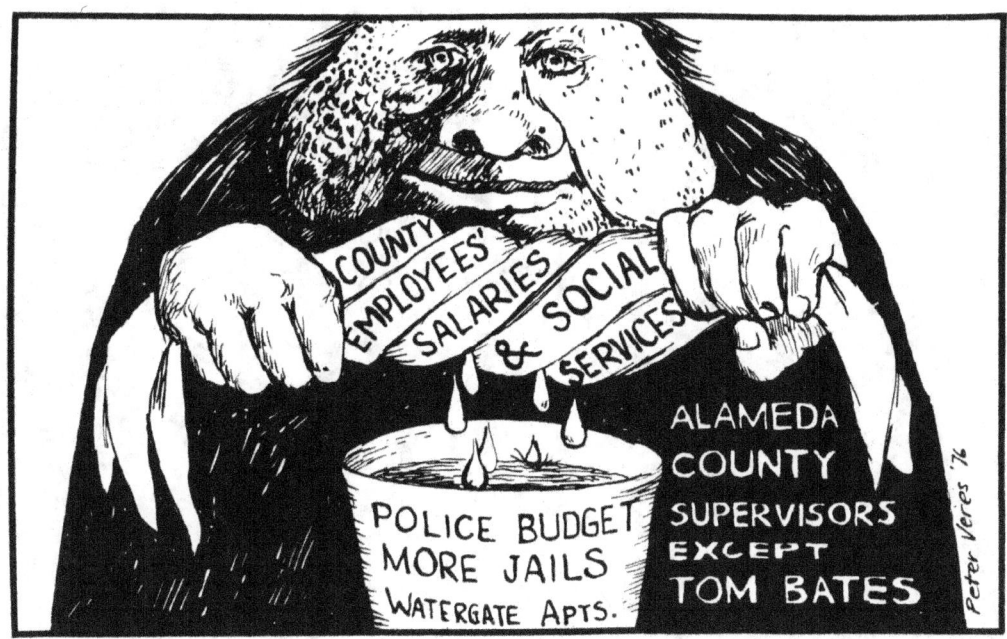

BREAD & JOBS, NOT CRUMBS & JAILS

The Alameda County Board of Supervisors, following the scenario of their counterparts in San Francisco and New York, are trying to make public employees the scapegoats for Alameda County's financial problems.

In current negotiations with County employees, the Board of Supervisors has used some familiar tactics: issued distorted statistics about employee wage levels, stonewalled union negotiations for one month putting forth their first positive proposal only after a large union demonstration, and then unilaterally passed a salary ordinance with dozens of different raises ranging from 0-13% and averaging 3.2% for rank-and-file employees. County employees have rejected these tactics and voted to strike.

While it seeks to blame public employees for causing property tax increases, the Board plans to spend more than $100 million over the next few years (without voter approval) for pre-trial detention facilities and courthouses.

Alameda County has the highest unemployment rate in California. Yet the Board uses "crime" to justify giving the largest increase in its $353 million budget to law enforcement departments. At the same time, hospitals, welfare offices, and libraries remain understaffed and their services are being quietly trimmed.

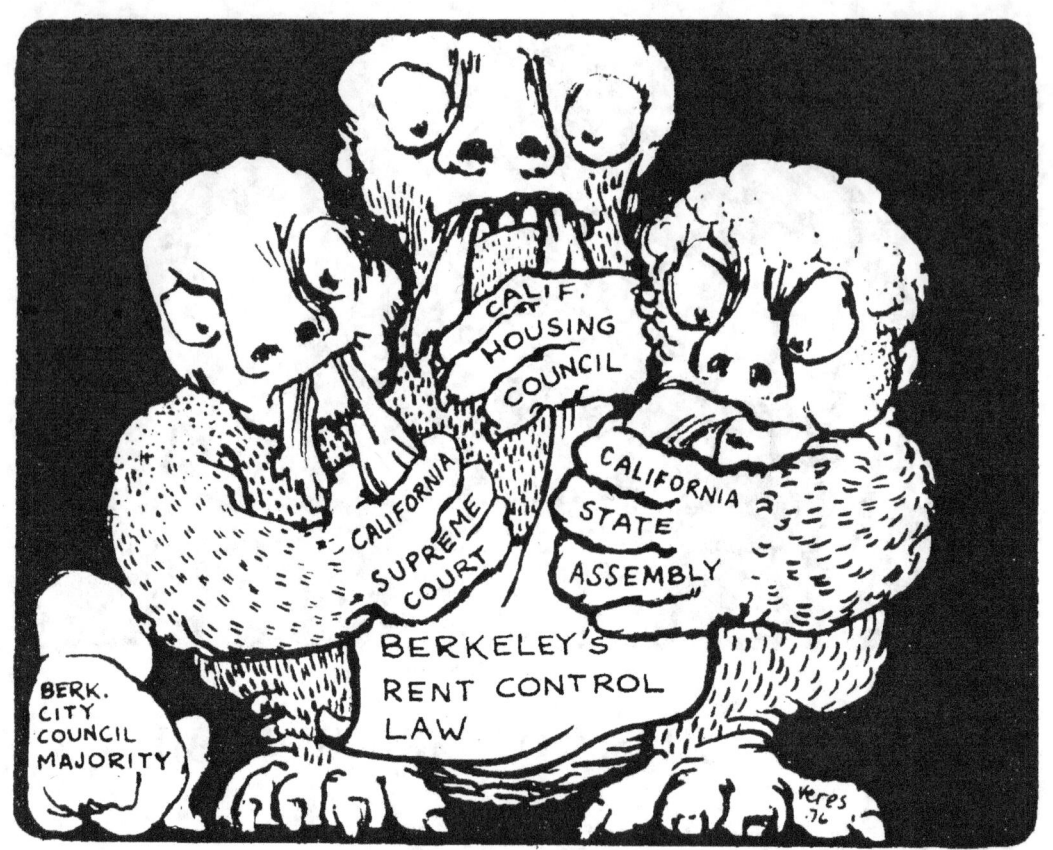

COURT, LEGISLATURE FLATTEN TENANTS

The week of June 14 was disastrous for tenants in Berkeley and in other cities around the state. Landlords were given the right by both the California Supreme Court and the state legislature to continue their extreme profiteering from people's needs for decent housing.

On June 16, the California Supreme Court decided the fate of Berkeley's Rent Control Charter Amendment. In a unanimous decision they ruled that the problems of landlords were more important than the needs of tenants.

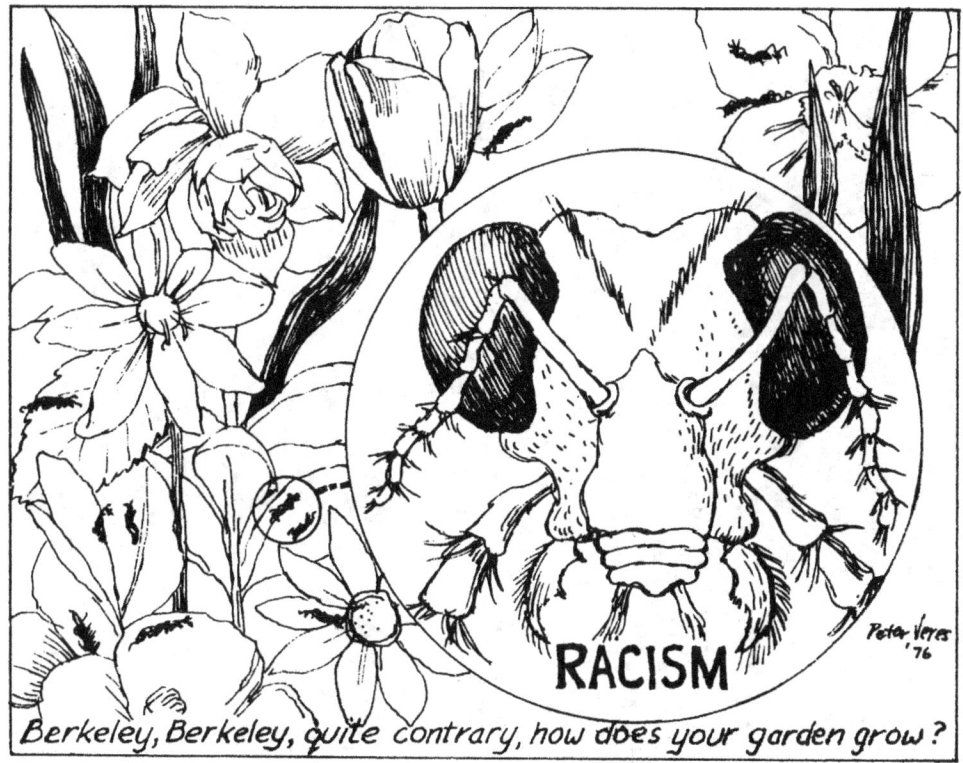

Berkeley, Berkeley, quite contrary, how does your garden grow?

RACISM IN OUR TOWN

The question of racism intimidates people. Our political and economic institutions continuously foster racism; it is useful to have a subgroup among workers. That gives the majority the comfort of knowing that they aren't on the bottom and it also allows for exploitation of those who are. But in times of economic crisis, exploitation of the majority as well becomes necessary — as witness budget reductions, service cutbacks, and layoffs: high premiums for profit-level insurance. It is in such times that we need a strong union of working people — all working people — to fight back. But how can we carry on that fight if we divert our efforts toward keeping down the sub-group? Exploiters know the value of racism for diluting our common fight!

But the racist thrust remains strong. Look at the problem in the schools. The board majority presents us with a choice: a racist policy of layoffs or financial disaster. But the belief that we can only solve the schools' money problems by laying off, by setting the seniority system against affirmative action, by encouraging conflict over jobs and integrated education between White and Third World workers, is specious, even dangerous. To ignore all other alternatives and only support the layoffs demonstrates a callous disregard for the need to build a multi-racial, progressive community in Berkeley. It is ironic that those "Progressives" who campaigned for racial equality, integration, and affirmative action are now quite willing to capitulate to "higher" priorities: fiscal responsibility and administrative integrity.

Let's take off our blinders. Racism is back in town — in fact, it never left. We must recognize it for what it is, strip away its various guises, and extirpate it. Berkeley will never be a united community until we do.

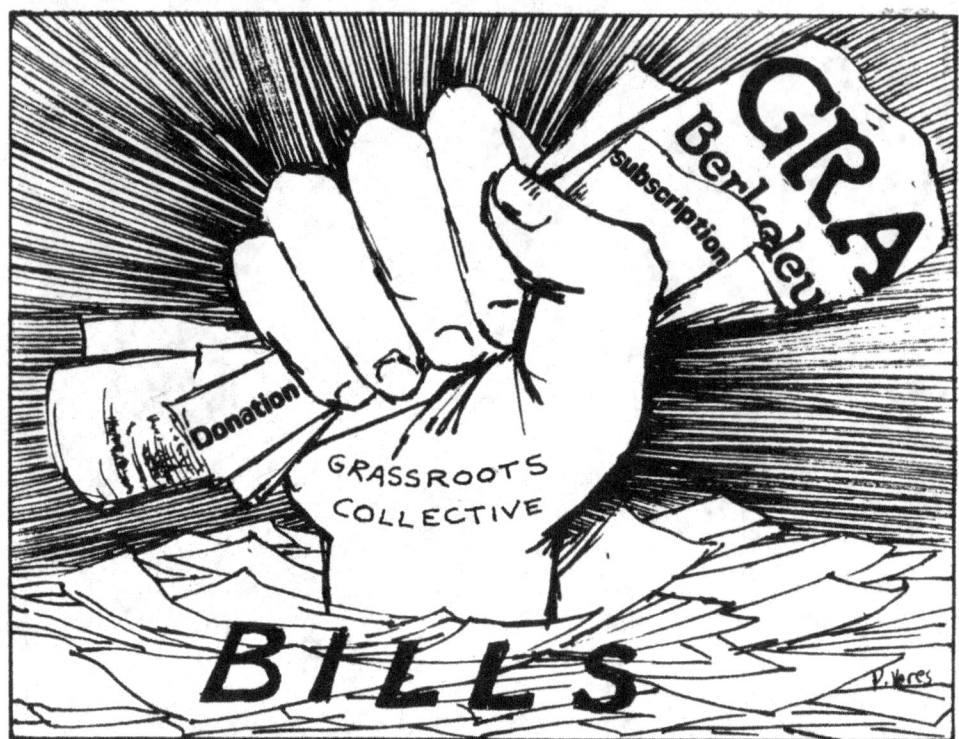

YOU GET WHAT YOU PAY FOR

After more than four years of regular publication, GRASSROOTS has become something of a fixture in Berkeley. For the collective, this status has both good and bad points. On the one hand, enough people consider us an important source of Berkeley news so we only have to scramble a little for the money to print each issue anymore. On the other hand, although we ARE growing, we aren't growing fast enough to do much more than we're already doing. We've reached a "comfortable" level and seem to be stuck there. We have neither the money nor the energy to do any more.

We feel that the Left in Berkeley is on the verge of a major breakthrough (a welcome change from the breakdowns we've suffered the past few years), and that GRASSROOTS is an important part of this. If we didn't, we wouldn't be putting so much time, money, and effort into the paper. But the collective hasn't, and can't, do it alone.

We know that there are a lot of you out there who read the paper and like it, but don't subscribe. We also know that there are a lot of you who want to do something meaningful, but haven't decided just what. So what it comes down to is this: If we had just 1000 more subscribers, we could enlarge the paper to provide more complete coverage of local affairs.

Now that Berkeley city policies can finally be turned in a progressive direction, communication of facts and ideas is more important than ever. The Berkeley Left has done a good job so far. A larger GRASSROOTS would be immeasurably better.

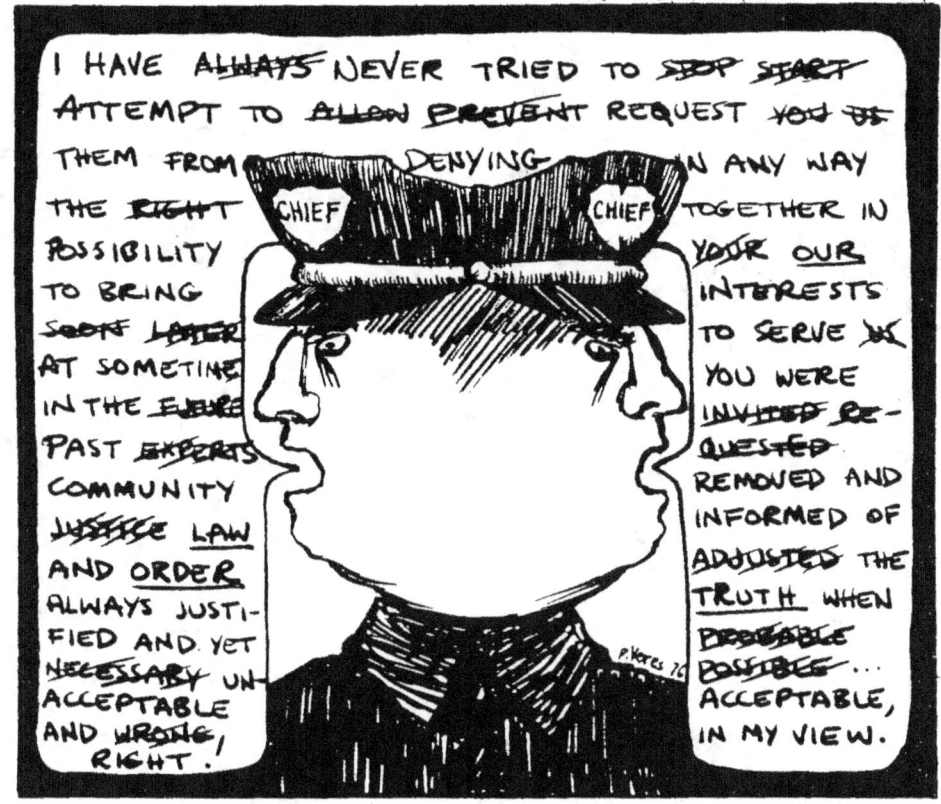

Acting Police Chief Ralph Schillinger is not to be believed. The BERKELEY BARB and the DAILY CALIFORNIAN have turned up some state military documents showing that the Berkeley Police Department (BPD) took part in some secret police-state training a few years ago. Schillinger received prominent mention as one of the speakers at an orientation session of the program, in 1970. Asked about it now, Schillinger replies. "I was not involved." That was a lie.

The Berkeley Police Officers Association — of which Schillinger is a member — has tied the Police Review Commission (PRC) up for months with a suit aimed at preventing the PRC from knowing what goes on at BPD hearings on citizen complaints. The courts finally decided in favor of the review board's right to be fully informed (see story, page 1). Schillinger assured PRC Chairperson Jim Chanin that there would be no further problems about the matter, but the information, by order of the acting chief, is still not forthcoming. Schillinger, a man of law, is flouting the PRC, a Commission which the voters established to oversee their police; he is, also flouting the Court in violation of his oath, and he is, in addition, lying to people about it.

Acting Chief Schillinger may be a good cop but he is not an honest man. Fire him.

Vol. V, No. 8   October 20–November 2, 1976

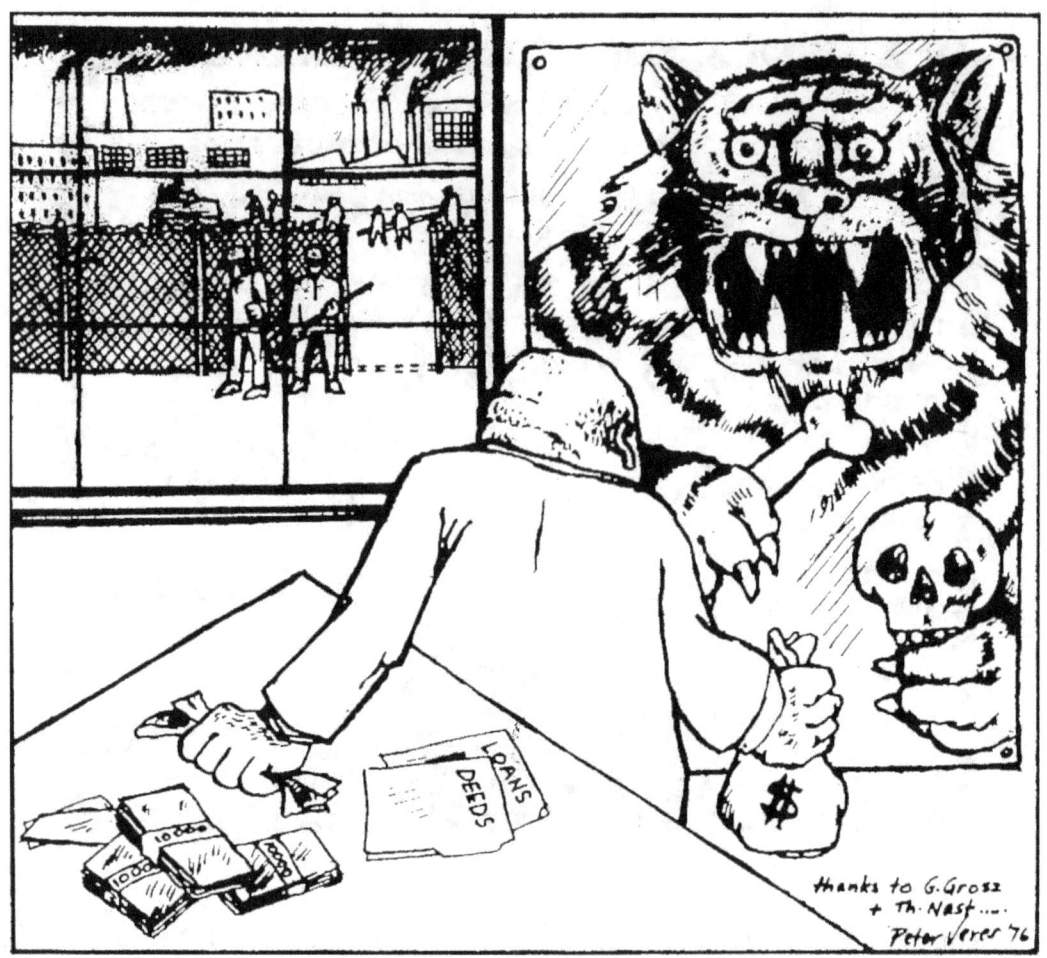

BRECHT : THE TIGER

This short story by Bertolt Brecht appears here for the first time in English.

In a great land there once lived a merchant. He bought all sorts of things, great and small, and sold them again at a very good profit. He bought factories and rivers, forests and neighborhoods, mines and ships. If people had nothing else to sell, he bought their time; that is, he allowed them to work for wages for him, and thus bought their muscles or their brain. He bought the grasp of their hands for his assembly lines, the force of their feet for his forges, their drawings and scripts for his account books.

He was a very great merchant and became an even greater one. Far and wide, he was highly esteemed, and he became even more esteemed. But then he got a dreadful illness.

My note says: thanks to G. Grosz + Th. Nast.... George Gross and Thomas Nast were great political cartoonists.

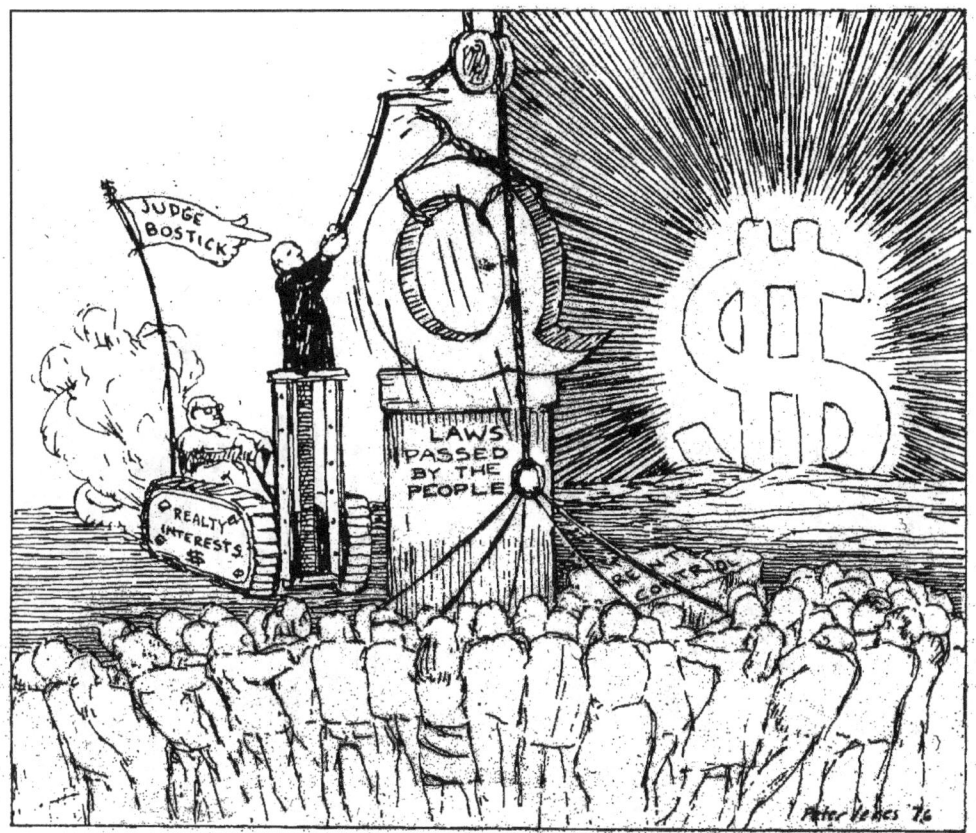

BOSTICK VERSUS THE PEOPLE... AGAIN!

the initiative process cannot undo what state, law – redevelopment law in this case – has done. In the same decision he declared moot a challenge to Proposition P. on grounds that the Council had properly exercised its powers to implement the law.

But wait a minute. The State's basic grant of governing powers to the City – our City Charter – has this to say: *"... voters... shall have power through the initiative ... to enact appropriate legislation to carry out and enforce any of the powers of the City or any of the powers of the Council."* (Article XIII, Section 92)

If the initiative process carries the same legislative power as the Council, as the Charter says it does, and if the Council can implement an initiative measure, as it has in the case of P. why can the initiative process not implement Q. without all this expensive legal bullshit?

Recall, it was Bostick who ruled against rent control on the same grounds – that voters cannot legislate by means of initiative. The Court of Appeals and the State Supreme Court disagreed with him, saying that it was perfectly reasonable for the voters to legislate as they had. Justice Bostick doesn't seem to learn.

Perhaps in the future, when initiative measures find their way into the courts – as they always seem to do – those defending the people's point of view would do well to

Vol. V, No. 10   November 17–December 7, 1976

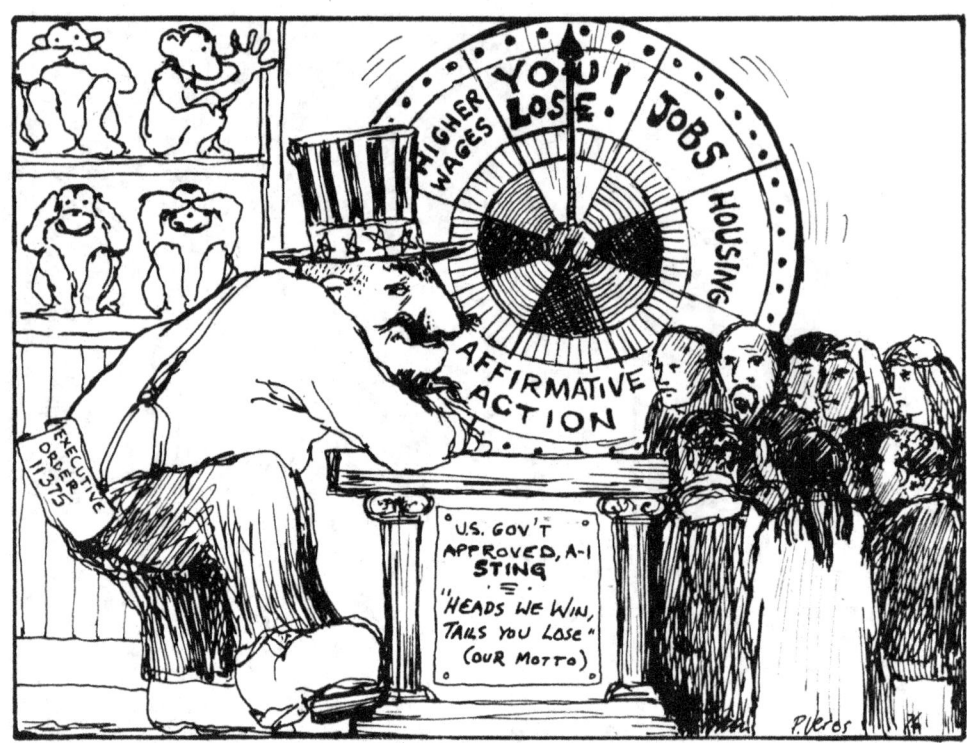

LATEST FEDERAL MOVE
AFFIRMATIVE ACTION ATTACKED

In the latest of a series of attacks against affirmative action, the Department of Labor has made several proposals which would effectively destroy the Federal Executive Order which forbids government contractors from discriminating in employment. The present order requires contractors to take affirmative action to compensate for the effects of past discrimination on the basis of race, color, national origin, religion, or sex.

The new proposal would significantly reduce the number of firms affected by the Executive Order; would require that employees who file complaints alleging discrimination must first appeal to the employer before appealing to the governmental agency; would impose additional standards on civil rights organizations who file class action complaints; would practically eliminate on-site inspection of contractors—the horror list goes on and on. The most revealing proposal would give the Director of the Office of Federal Contract Compliance Programs the power to exempt a contractor from an affirmative action program if measures against the contractor would affect the "national interest" or if the contractor had "unique characteristics."

We need hundreds of letters to protest these proposals and to demand that public hearings be held in the Bay Area before any changes take place. Write to: Mr. Lawrence Z. Lorber
   Director, Office of Federal Contract Compliance Programs
   U.S. Department of Labor
   Washington, D.C. 20210

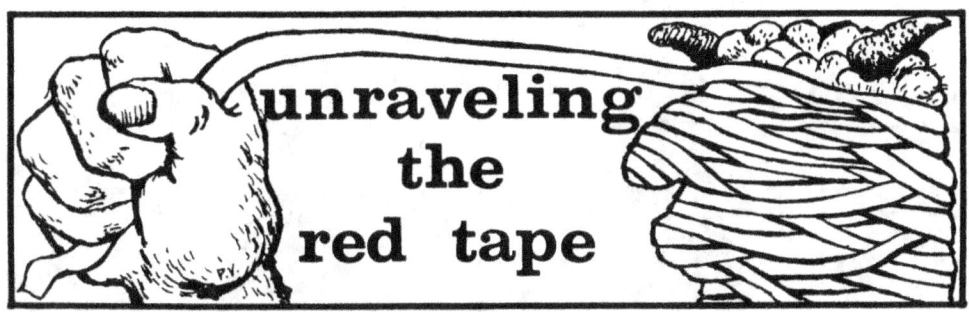

This was a new column dealing with questions about unemployment benefits, who is qualified and how to apply for it, and how to overcome the difficulties of getting one's claims paid. The piece gave a phone number for the Pro Per Collective, which must have contributed the column.

Vol. V, No. 11   December 8–21, 1976

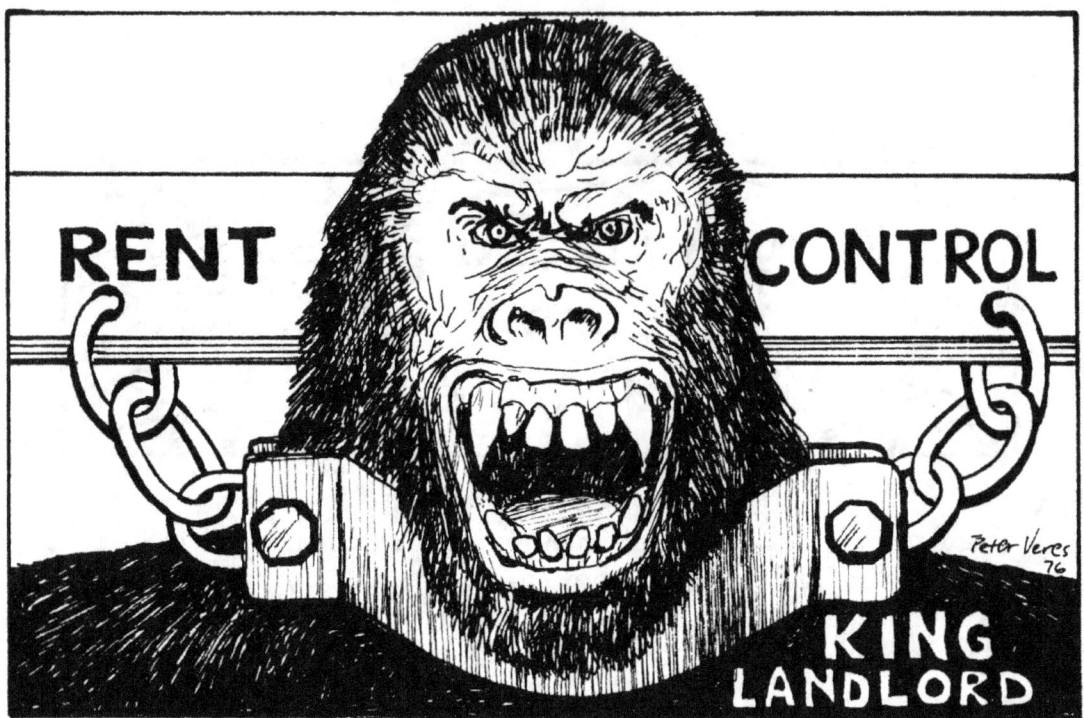

PUT RENT CONTROL ON THE BALLOT

If you rent, you probably received a rent increase recently. Some renters around town have checked their landlords' property tax assessments to discover their rents have increased disproportionately to the amount of their landlords' tax hikes. While inflation has hit other housing costs, a strong feeling prevails that many landlords are tacking on exorbitant rents and pointing to property taxes as an excuse. This isn't new.

The situation cries out for a remedy, especially in these times of high unemployment and inflation. An initiative for a rent control charter amendment is circulating right now. We urge everyone to sign and circulate the petition, and to let friends and neighbors know about the campaign.

EXTRAVAGANT CLAIMS FORTHCOMING

Don't be put off by the extravagant claims made by opponents of rent control. The initiative has been written to comply with the State Supreme Court's ruling which threw out the 1972 rent control charter amendment passed by Berkeley voters. But the court also declared that rent control is not unconstitutional.

This is a bit of an over-the-top drawing, and unfair to King Kong since he was more victim than perpetrator, captured and chained by unscrupulous profiteers. Sorry, Kong. And certainly not all of Berkeley landlords were exploiters.

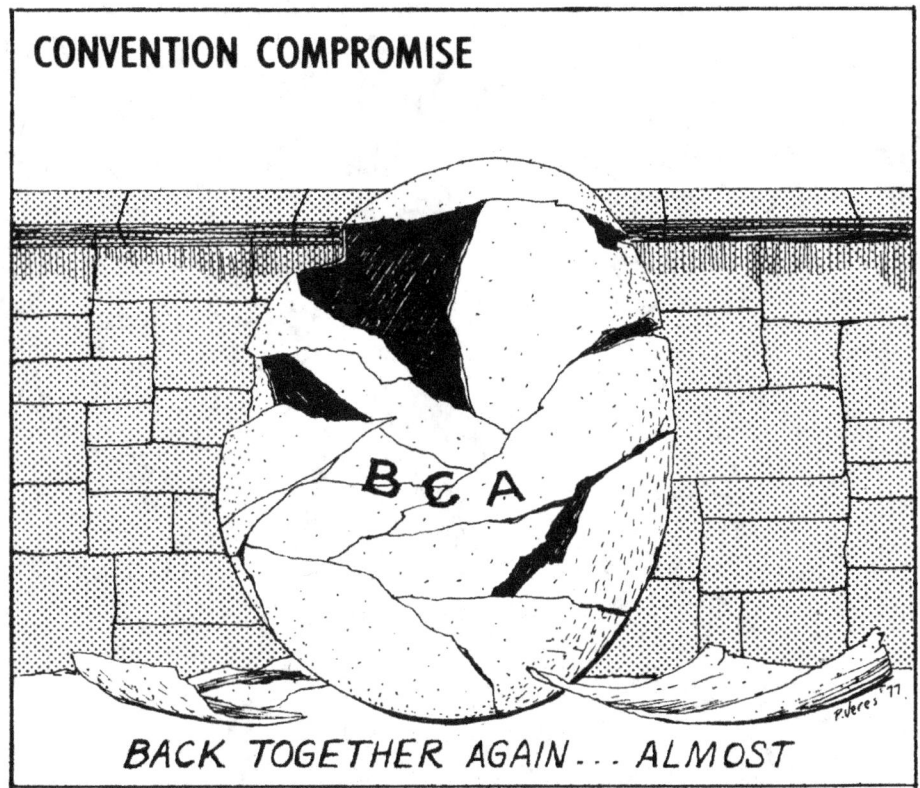

Berkeley Citizens Action has selected a slate of three candidates to run for city council in April, leaving the fourth slot unfilled. The agreement followed two days of conflict which nearly spelled the end of the coalition. Disaster was avoided because in the eleventh hour issues which had not been openly discussed were finally brought before the convention. The discussion helped clear the air of underlying rumors and accusation which led to the stalemate.

The central issue was Mark Allen's membership in the Communist Party, but a majority of participants could not understand why this alone would eliminate him from a coalition slate. Many were confused by the Third World Caucus's reversal of their support for Allen and by Ying Lee Kelley's and Margot Dashiell's adamant refusal to include him on the slate.

The compromise, proposed by Margot Dashiell, was made in the spirit of unity to allow people to work for both the BCA slate and Mark Allen without working against either one. This was acceptable to Allen, who had played a calming role during some of the more angry moments in the discussion.

While the compromise saved the coalition this time, it provides no long-term answers. The issues raised need thorough and open discussion. Some of the questions raised are:

What is the purpose of the coalition? Is it solely electoral politics or does it go beyond that?

Can the coalition include the Communist and other left parties? Can liberal Democrats, social democrats, communists and other Marxists ever coalesce?

What stake do working class and trade union people have in our coalition? How do the Third World communities relate to it?

Vol. V, No. 15   February 9–22, 1977

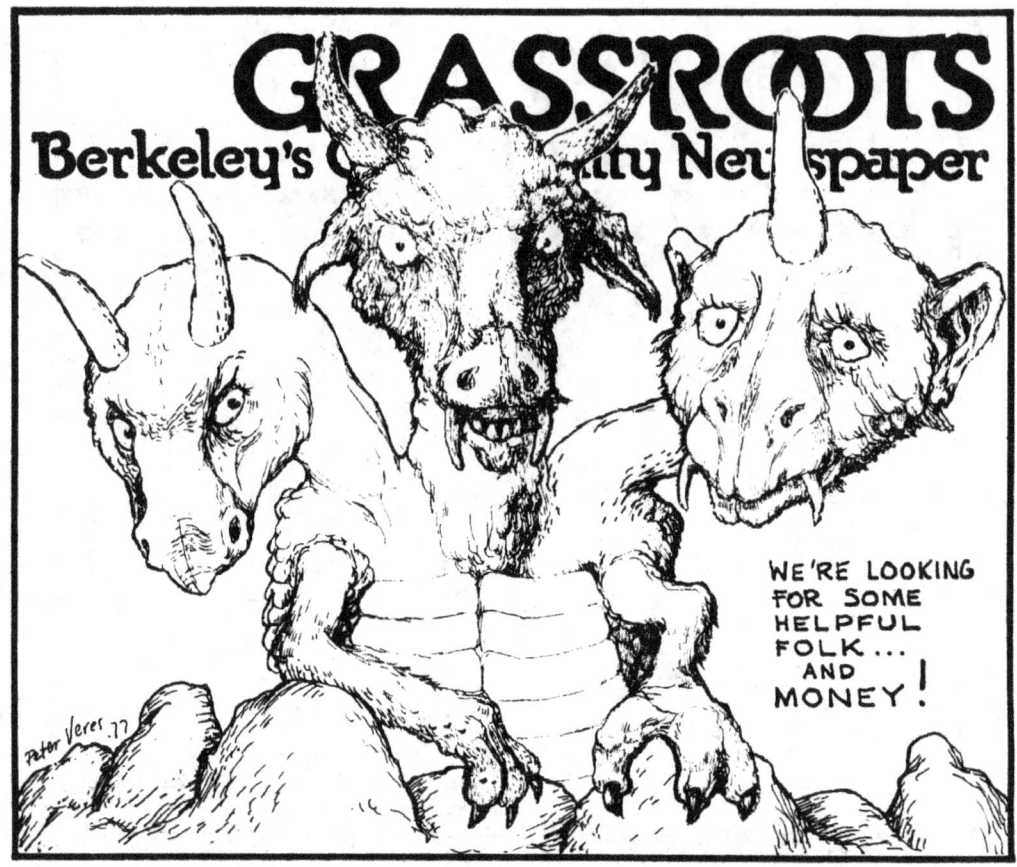

THE MOON BELONGS TO EVERYONE... BUT
SUBSCRIPTIONS ARE FIVE BUCKS A YEAR

GRASSROOTS belongs to the people of Berkeley. This is our biggest asset and, ironically, our biggest deficit. On one hand it means that everybody in the community has access to the paper, not just those who can afford to advertise. It is not accidental that the Oceanview Committee publicized much of its struggle in these pages. On the other hand, being a community newspaper means we don't have very much money. We can't pay salaries to reporters or business managers or office staff. We don't pay people to paste up the paper, repair the newsracks, type our copy, sweep the floors, or answer the phone. All this is done by volunteers, people like you and me who have a commitment to radical change. Every cent we get in goes for typesetting, printing, mailing, and rent. This comes to about a thousand bucks a month.

We would like to see some more signs of your support. We would like you to send us some money or we would like you to work on the paper. Let's take up the money thing first. We want to be able to print at least a 12-page issue every time. We have the copy; we don't always have the bread. Many of you read the paper but don't subscribe. If you would subscribe, we would have the bread. Eighty percent of our income comes from subscriptions. Do we hear eighty five?

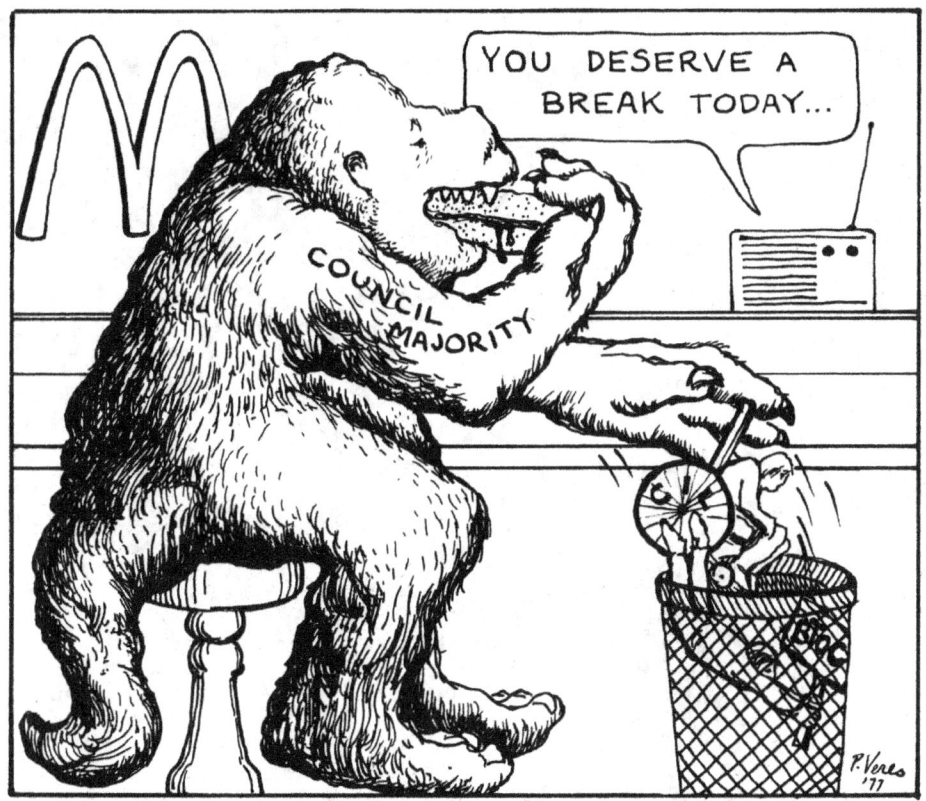

VINDICTIVE COUNCIL SLAMS TENANTS AND DISABLED

Something over 60% of the residents of Berkeley rent their homes. That involves some kind of relationship with a landlord/lady, or that person's representative. That relationship can be mellow, but all too often it isn't. All too often the person who owns the property is interested in profit and could care less about the families who pay that profit. That is why an organization like the Berkeley Tenants' Organizing Committee (BTOC) is important. It is the only organization in the city which helps people who rent with the problems involved in renting: arbitrary evictions, unpaid deposits, poor maintenance of the living quarters, etc. The people of this city need BTOC; the city should support BTOC.

The city should also support the Center for Independent Living (CIL). The Center has pioneered one program after another aimed at making it possible for disabled people to live full, independent lives, to cope with the world on their own rather than stagnating in hospitals or other institutions.

Yet a majority of our city council voted, at their March 15 meeting (see related story) *not* to fund BTOC and to leave CIL *without* funds for a program of housing assistance for disabled people. That might make some sense if the city were providing such services, but of course the city is not. Their money goes for other things, usually in support, directly or indirectly, of business. The council majority is not about to do anything in support of the people of the city or of the community agencies which meet some of their needs.

The council majority's action is mean and petty, especially given the relatively small sums involved, but it is more than that; it is a direct affront to the people of Berkeley, a slap in the face for people with real, unmet needs and for people who are working hard to try and fill those needs. It is a disgusting show.

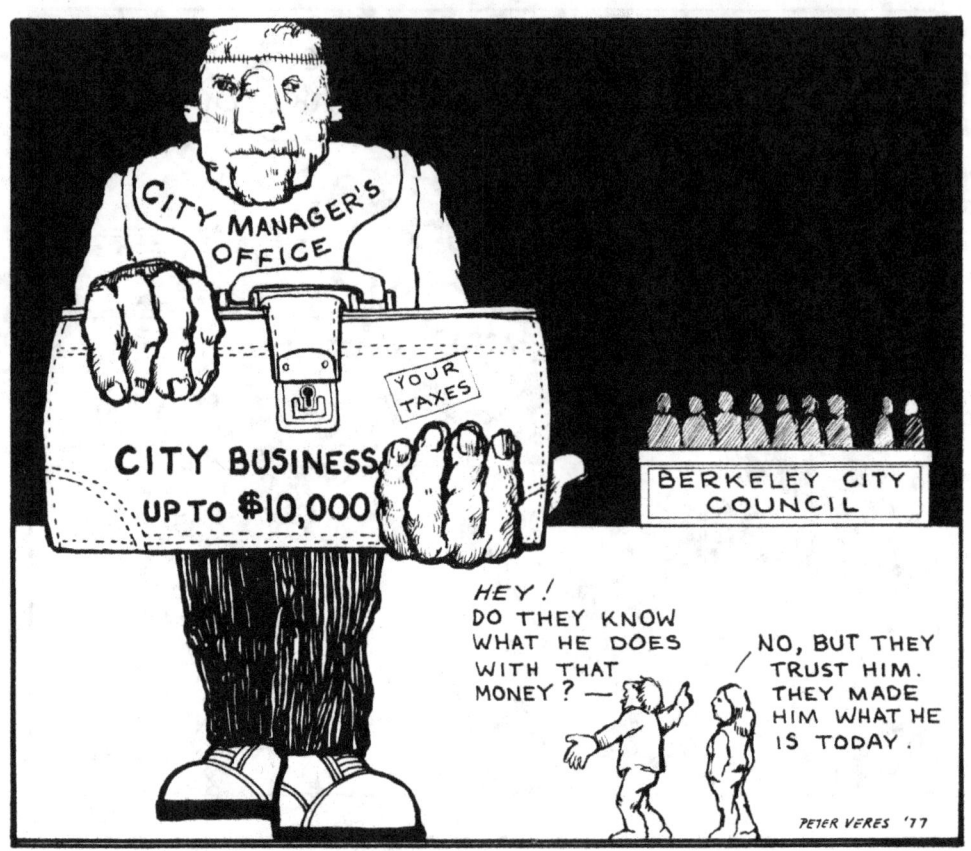

COUNCIL HIDES EXPENDITURES

Applying its usual nearsightedness the Berkeley City Council has voted to allow City Manager Elijah Rogers power to spend up to $10,000 without council approval. Voters removed the City Charter's $3,000 upper limit on the City Manager's freedom to spend through passage of Measure A on April 19. The measure mandated the council to set the upper limit from now on.

Passage of the $10,000 limit (and a $15,000 limit for "emergencies") ushers in a new era of municipal cover-up of where our tax money goes. Many times in the past serious problems have cropped up even in small expenditures. For example, a firm giving pap smears was once found to have a poor accuracy record in its tests. Councilmembers were able to catch the problem, but if granted now — as the contract would be beneath the $10,000 limit — no knowledge of the company, of what it is doing, or who it is doing it to would be available.

The justification for the new limit is to save money on paper and staff time. City Manager Rogers estimates the savings at $44,000 a year. We support efforts to save money through economies, but not at the expense of curtailing knowledge about where tax money is going. We support an alternative proposal which would set a $6,000 limit, with all expenditures below that to be included on a list presented to the council, avoiding the heavy paperwork involved when funding requests go to the council.

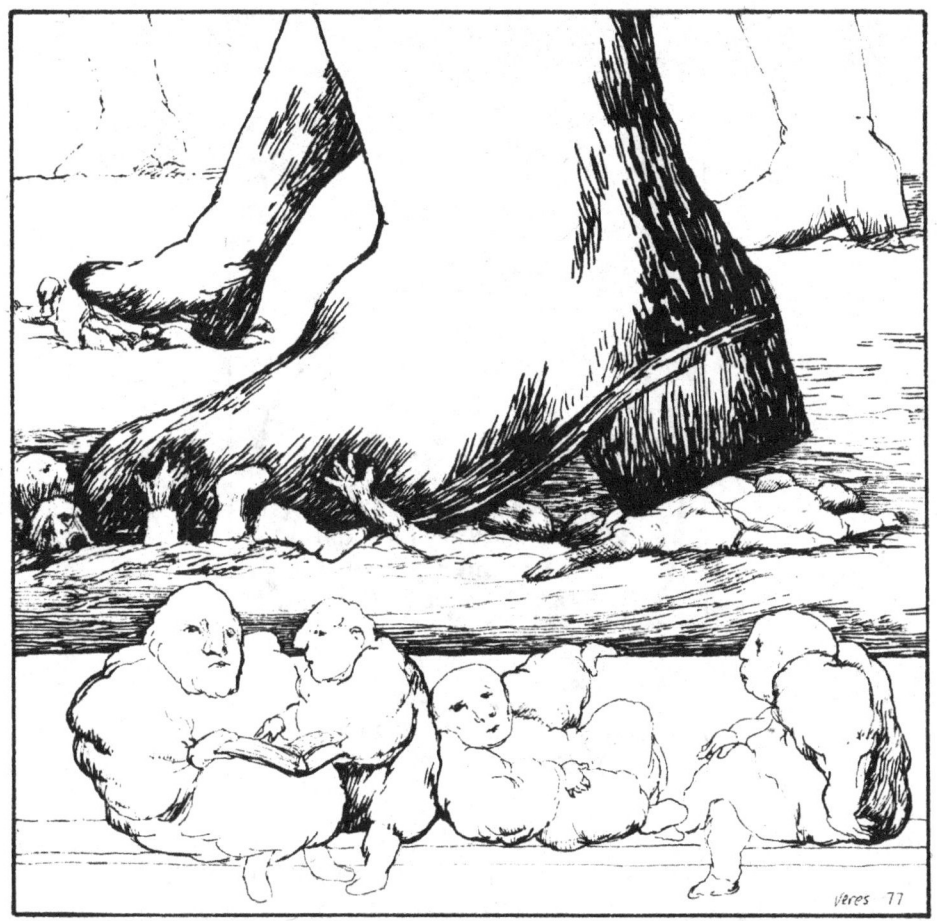

WIDENER ON APARTHEID... DON'T ROCK THE BOAT

We are astonished and disgusted by some of the statements we heard at the most recent city council meeting. At issue was a request by Campuses United Against Apartheid (CUAA), a student group, for a city council resolution calling on the District Attorney to drop charges against 58 people arrested at a recent Sproul Hall sit-in. The demonstration was a protest against the University of California's support of South Africa's racist regime. Our council turned the students down. Councilmembers Sue Hone and William Segesta both feel that it would be "inappropriate" for the council to honor such a request. Neither one explained why they hold such peculiar views, but Hone called it lobbying and said that the council should only do that with Congresspeople. Segesta said he would make up for his lack of support by volunteering as a defense attorney. Our thought is that CUAA doesn't need friends like that.

THE MAYOR

But the worst came from the Mayor. His position is that the only correct approach is to persuade the boards of directors of the various companies — who are making millions by working South African Blacks for long hours at low pay in unsafe, almost inhuman conditions — to institute affirmative action hiring and promotion policies with equal pay for Blacks and Whites in their South African operations.

Vol. VI, No. 6   September 28–October 11, 1977

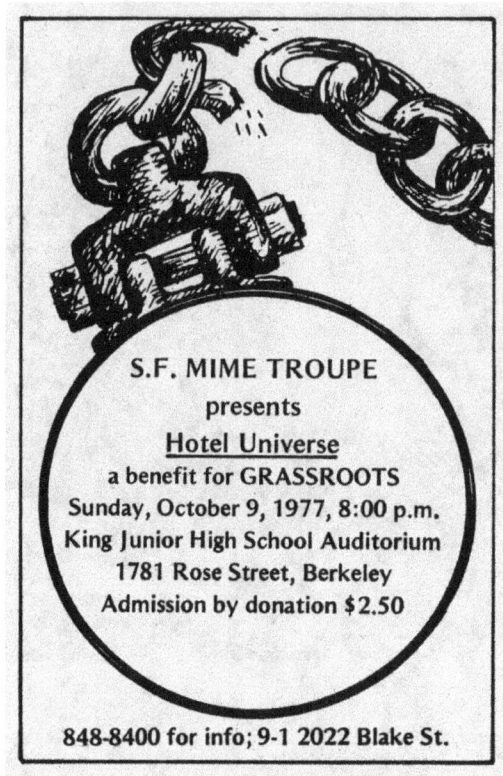

This ad was for the Mime Troupe's 1977 summer show, which was, as all their shows for the past 50 years or more, performed free in the parks of the Bay Area and beyond. Hotel Universe was based on the real-life story of the mostly Filipino tenants of the International Hotel in San Francisco, who struggled for seven years against the inevitable, the destruction of their residence to make way for "urban renewal". Before the show's San Francisco opening, that struggle ended in a mass eviction of the 196 tenants by the city. The Hotel stood vacant for years, was then demolished, and the site remained an empty hole until 2005 when a new apartment building for senior housing was completed.

My drawing combines the image of a wrecking ball and a prisoner's ball and chain. The breaking chain frees both the threatened Hotel and its poor, powerless tenant "prisoners" from eviction.

Vol. VI, No. 13 January 11–24, 1978

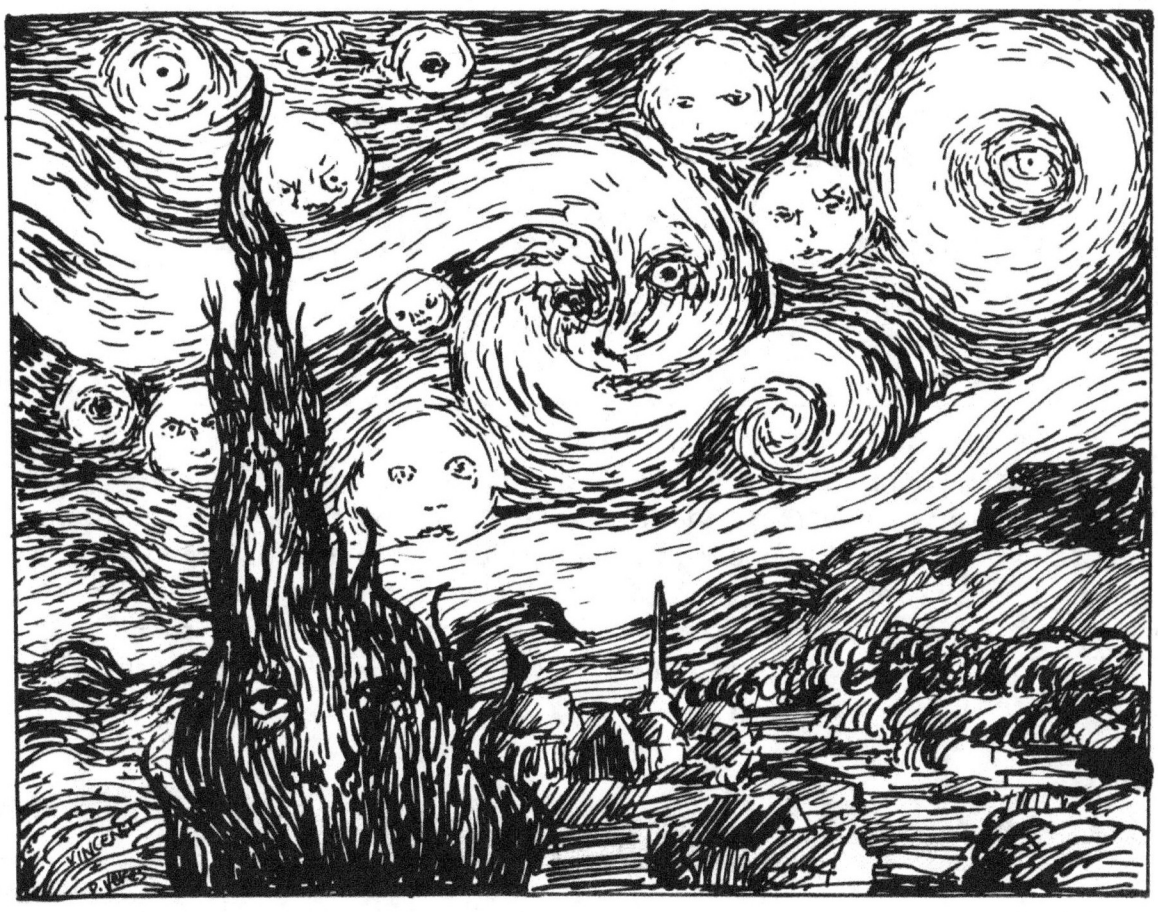

I drew on the vision of Vincent Van Gogh to illustrate a review of the movie *Close Encounters of the Third Kind*, a sci-fi vision of Steven Spielberg.

Vol. VI, No. 10   November 23–December 6, 1977

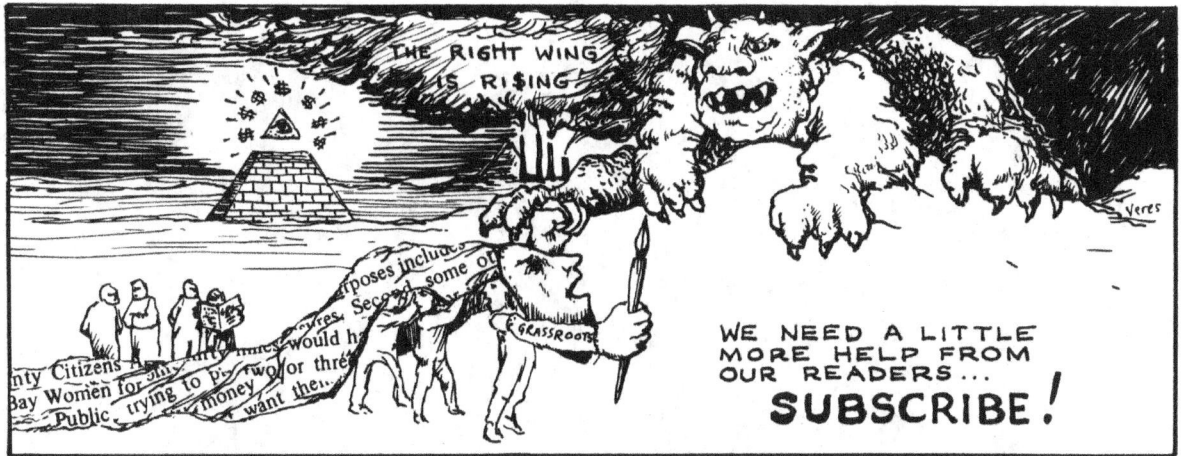

A GOOD PAPER IS HARD TO FIND

Every now and then we get low on money so we print an appeal for more funds. We did that about three months ago and received donations amounting to over a thousand dollars. We are extremely gratified when something like that happens, but the sad fact is that that money is now gone. We spent every dime of it on putting out this paper.

So once again we have to come back to the community with our hands out. You know that we are providing a service which Berkeley needs, a service which nobody else provides. We know that when we come asking, we can count on somebody to come through for us, to send us the bucks we need to keep the paper on the streets.

But we also know that such a procedure is unfair. It lays the burden on a few of our supporters, those who find themselves with some extra bucks just when we're asking for it. There's an easier way, a more collective way to do it: more subscribers.

ONLY 700 MORE

If only 700 more readers would reach into their pockets for the modest five bucks we ask for a year's subscription, we would be home free. We could put out the paper without the constantly diminishing bank balance that is our present lot. We could turn our energies to fuller, more comprehensive news coverage, to investigative stories, to following up on the many issues we're unable to completely cover. We could give you much, much more of what you look to GRASSROOTS to find.

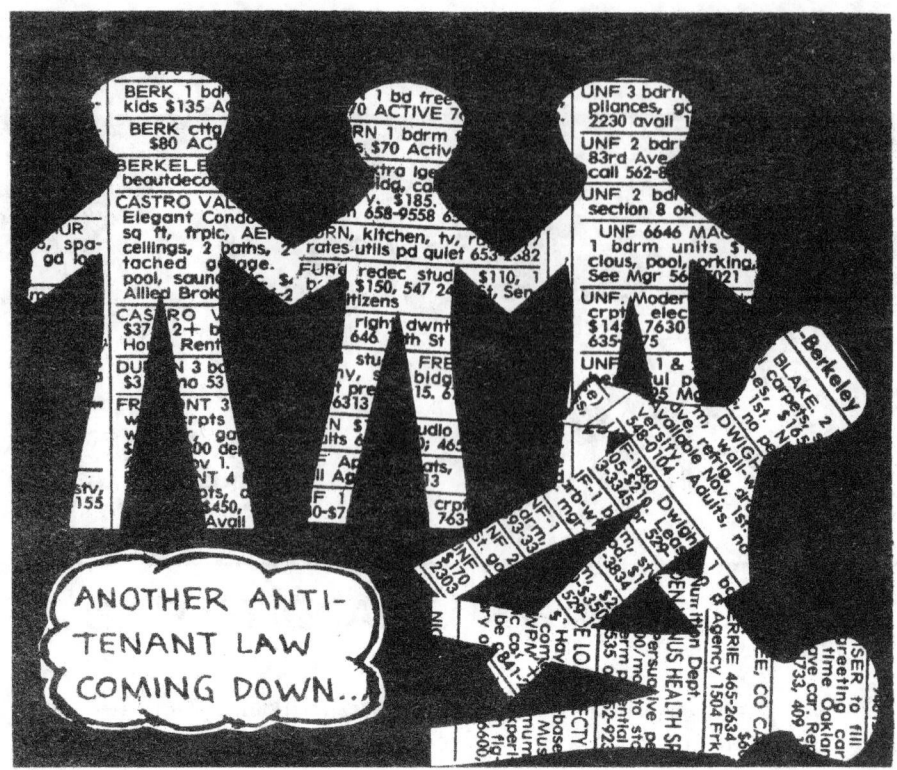

MEETING HEARS OUTRAGE OVER ZONING REVISIONS

An overflow crowd of more than 200 jammed into the meeting room of the University Lutheran Chapel on Thursday, November 17, to voice their overwhelming opposition to several proposed revisions to the Zoning Ordinance and to offer their energy in gaining support for a public hearing on these proposals.

Many in the audience expressed the belief that the proposal which would limit to three the number of unrelated adults who may live together (more than three would require a use permit) was aimed at those who seek alternative living arrangements, people who were not acceptable in certain parts of the community. Some felt that the move was tied to real estate interests which would profit from a tighter housing market. Others expressed their fears that if this proposal passes, they will have to move because there would be more than three unrelated persons in their household. As one participant said, "I would have to tell my landlady, a widow who has lived in her

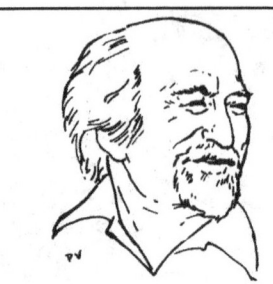

from left field
Ray Pinkson

In his columns Ray Pinkson related stories from his long politically active past to current issues and situations. In this first one he talks about the movie *Julia*, about an American woman's work in the anti-Nazi underground in Austria before the outbreak of WW II, and of his own possible arrest on a train near the German border while carrying a New York magazine with "a large cartoon depicting Hitler as a mad beast trying to swallow all of Europe". He decided to eat the page before he was found with it. An instructive story about the potential of political cartoons.